UNLOCK YOUR INNER SUPERHERO

PRACTICAL STEPS FOR HOLISTIC LIVING & PERSONAL MASTERY

AMIT AGARWAL

INDIA • SINGAPORE • MALAYSIA

ISBN

Hardcase 979-8-89610-331-8
Paperback 979-8-89588-613-7

ACKNOWLEDGMENTS

This book is the culmination of a journey I could not have completed alone. First and foremost, I want to thank my mother, whose unwavering love and belief in me have been my guiding light. To my two sisters, who have always supported me through thick and thin, your encouragement has been my strength. To my father, my true real-life superhero, thank you for teaching me the value of hard work and perseverance—your lessons continue to shape my path.

To my incredible wife, Esha, your patience, love, and understanding have made all of this possible. And to my daughter, Vihaana, you are my inspiration every day, reminding me of the joy and beauty that life holds.

Thank you all for being my pillars of strength. This book is as much yours as it is mine.

TABLE OF CONTENTS

Preface 7
Introduction: Is This Book for You? 9
Why This Book? 11
How to Use This Book 15
A Personal Invitation 19

Introduction **21**
Chapter 01 The Journey to Abundance 23

Section 1: Mindset and Mental Health **29**
Chapter 02 The Power of Mindset 31
Chapter 03 The Power of Reflection, Self-Awareness and Healing 39

Section 2: Physical Health and Wellness **47**
Chapter 04 Physical Health – The Foundation of a Fulfilling Life 49
Chapter 05 Embracing Wellness – Physical, Mental, and Emotional Health 55
Chapter 06 Building Healthy Habits 61

Section 3: Relationships and Community **67**
Chapter 07 Building and Maintaining Meaningful Relationships 69
Chapter 08 The Importance of Community 75

Section 4: Goal Setting and Personal Growth **81**
Chapter 09 Setting Clear Goals and Finding Your Path 83
Chapter 10 Living with Purpose 89
Chapter 11 Mastering the Art of Decision Making 94

Section 5: Balance Work and Time Management **101**

Chapter 12 Achieving Balance Between Work and Life 103

Chapter 13 Mastering Time Management for a Productive Life 109

Chapter 14 The Importance of Audit and Review 116

Section 6: Productivity and Proactivity **125**

Chapter 15 Overcoming Procrastination 127

Chapter 16 Developing Systems for Success 137

Chapter 17 Responding vs. Reacting to Situations 145

Section 7: Gratitude and Growth **153**

Chapter 18 The Power of Gratitude 155

Chapter 19 Continuous Learning and Personal Growth 161

Section 8: Skills for Success **169**

Chapter 20 The Art of Delegation 171

Chapter 21 The Power of Saying No 178

Chapter 22 The Power of Doing Nothing 185

Conclusion **191**

Chapter 23 Conclusion – Embrace Your Inner Superhero 193

About the Author *199*

PREFACE

Welcome to *Unlock Your Inner Superhero: Practical Steps for Holistic Living and Personal Mastery*. This book is the culmination of years of personal experience, research, and a deep desire to help others unleash their full potential. It is designed to guide you on a transformative journey towards a more fulfilling, balanced, and abundant life.

Throughout my own journey, I have encountered numerous challenges and setbacks. Yet, each obstacle has offered valuable lessons and opportunities for growth. This book is my way of sharing those lessons with you, offering practical advice and actionable steps to help you navigate your path to self-discovery and empowerment.

Ask yourself: What matters to you most? What problem do you want to solve? What change do you want to bring about? Your purpose should resonate deeply with your aspirations, values, and hopes.

Whether you are seeking to improve your physical health, enhance your mental wellbeing, strengthen your relationships, or achieve your personal and professional goals, this book provides the tools and insights you need to succeed. I hope that by reading this book, you will feel inspired to discover your inner strengths and live a life of purpose, passion, and abundance.

By the end of this book, you will have a comprehensive understanding of how to live a balanced and fulfilling life.

Remember, heroes aren't born – they're created. It's the choices we make, the causes we champion, and the people we inspire that define us.

Thank you for allowing me to be part of your journey. It's time to unleash your inner superhero!

"Your greatest superpower is not strength or speed—it's the ability to believe in your own potential."

– Amit Agarwal
Your Guide to Greatness

INTRODUCTION: IS THIS BOOK FOR YOU?

Do you feel stuck in life, like you're capable of much more but unsure how to harness that potential? Do you find yourself overwhelmed by daily demands, struggling to find balance and fulfilment? If these questions resonate with you, then this book is for you.

This book is your guide to discovering the extraordinary potential that lies within you and transforming your life through holistic practices. Here, you'll find actionable steps, inspiring stories, and practical advice designed to help you master every aspect of your life.

Who Should Read This Book?

This book is designed for anyone seeking to improve their quality of life and become the best version of themselves. Whether you're at the beginning of your self-improvement journey or looking to refine and enhance your current practices, this book offers practical guidance and actionable steps to help you achieve greatness!

Those Feeling Stuck or Unmotivated

Individuals Seeking Balance and Fulfilment

People Interested in Holistic Living

Professionals and Entrepreneurs

Those Seeking Personal Growth and Continuous Learning

Anyone Looking to Enhance Their Relationships

A Call to Action

If you see yourself in any of the descriptions above, this book is meant for you. It's time to take charge of your life, harness your full potential, and embark on a journey of self-discovery and transformation. This is not just a book – it's a guide to becoming your own superhero.

"The only thing standing between you and the life you want is the story you tell yourself. Change the story, and you change your reality."

– Author

WHY THIS BOOK?

In our fast-paced world, we are constantly bombarded with challenges, distractions, and pressures that can leave us feeling drained and disconnected. It's easy to lose sight of our goals and forget the incredible power we hold within ourselves. This book aims to reignite that power, guiding you on a journey of self-discovery and personal growth.

Being a superhero doesn't mean you need to wear a cape or save the world in a single day. Your "superpower" might be as simple as resilience—the ability to get back up after a tough day—or the courage to face everyday challenges with determination. Maybe it's the strength to set boundaries, or the patience to make slow, steady progress toward a personal goal. For some, a superpower might be empathy, showing kindness and support to others even when life is difficult.

The idea of being a superhero is about tapping into these everyday strengths—qualities you already possess—and using them to improve your life and the lives of those around you. Whether it's getting through a stressful workday or making time for self-care, your powers are already at play. This book will help you recognise and harness them more intentionally.

What You Will Gain from This Book

By reading this book, you will:

- **Develop a Growth Mindset**: Learn how to shift your thinking to embrace challenges and opportunities for growth.
- **Build Healthy Habits**: Create routines and systems that support your physical, mental, and emotional well-being.

- **Overcome Procrastination**: Discover effective strategies to stop delaying and start taking action towards your goals.
- **Manage Stress and Anxiety**: Learn techniques to maintain inner peace and balance, even in the face of adversity.
- **Mindfulness and Gratitude**: Learn about the power of mindfulness and gratitude in enhancing your overall happiness and contentment.
- **Time Management and Balance**: Master time management skills to increase productivity and maintain a balanced life.
- **Enhance Your Relationships**: Improve your communication skills and build meaningful connections with others.
- **Foster Continuous Growth**: Embrace lifelong learning and personal development to keep evolving and thriving.

What You Will Find in This Book

This book is structured to provide a comprehensive toolkit for holistic living and personal mastery. Here's what you can expect:

- **Actionable Steps**: Each chapter is designed to offer practical advice and clear, actionable steps that you can implement immediately. Whether it's building healthy habits, managing stress, or enhancing relationships, you'll find strategies that are easy to apply in your daily life.
- **Inspiring Stories**: Throughout the book, you'll encounter real-life stories of individuals who have overcome limiting beliefs and challenges to unlock their full potential. These stories serve as inspiration and provide valuable lessons on resilience, determination, and growth.
- **Practical Advice**: The book is filled with practical advice on various aspects of life, from physical health and mental wellbeing to spiritual growth. Each chapter provides insights and tools that are relevant and useful.
- **Reflection and Exercises**: To help you apply the concepts, each chapter includes reflection questions and exercises. These are designed to encourage self-awareness and help you track your progress on your journey to becoming your own champion.

Why This Approach Works

The combination of actionable steps, inspiring stories, and practical advice is designed to be engaging and motivating. By breaking down complex concepts into manageable steps, the book makes it easier for you to implement changes and see real progress. The reflection questions and exercises ensure that you actively engage with the content, making the journey of personal growth a dynamic and interactive process.

"True power comes from within. It's the courage to keep going when the path gets tough."

– Author

HOW TO USE THIS BOOK

To fully benefit from its content, it's important to understand how to navigate and utilise the resources and exercises provided. It is essential to approach this book with an open mind and a willingness to take action. This chapter provides you with a roadmap on how to navigate the book, utilise the tools provided, and implement the teachings effectively in your life.

Setting Your Intentions

Before diving into the book, take a moment to set your intentions. Reflect on what you hope to achieve by reading this book. Whether it's improving your physical health, enhancing your mental wellbeing, or finding a better work-life balance, having clear intentions will guide your journey and keep you focused.

This Book is Structured to Guide You

Here's how you can make the most of your journey through self-discovery and personal growth:

1. **Approach Each Chapter with an Open Mind**
    - **Be Open to New Ideas**: The concepts and practices discussed in this book may be new to you. Approach each chapter with an open mind, ready to learn and grow.
    - **Reflect on Your Current Situation**: As you read, think about how each topic applies to your life. Personal reflection is key to transformation.

2. **Engage with the Content Actively**

    - **Take Notes**: Jot down key insights, quotes, and ideas that resonate with you. This will reinforce the concepts and serve as a quick reference later.
    - **Highlight Important Sections**: Use a highlighter to mark passages that you find particularly inspiring or relevant to your goals.

3. **Implement Practical Steps**

    - **Actionable Advice**: Each chapter includes practical steps and actionable advice. Don't just read them – implement these steps in your daily life.
    - **Start Small**: Begin with small, manageable changes. Gradually incorporate more practices as you grow comfortable with each step.

4. **Reflect and Exercise**

    - **Ask Yourself**: At the end of each chapter, you'll find reflection questions. Take time to answer these thoughtfully, as they are designed to deepen your understanding and help you apply the concepts.
    - **Time to Take Action**: Engage in the exercises provided. These are practical activities meant to reinforce what you've learnt and help you integrate new habits into your life.

5. **Track Your Progress**

    - **Keep a Journal**: Maintaining a journal throughout this journey can be incredibly beneficial. Record your thoughts, progress, challenges, and successes.
    - **Set Milestones**: Break down your goals into smaller milestones. Celebrate each achievement, no matter how small, to stay motivated.

6. **Revisit Chapters as Needed**

    - **Continuous Learning**: Personal growth is an ongoing process. Revisit chapters that you found particularly challenging or relevant. Each read can offer new insights and reinforce your learning.
    - **Adapt and Adjust**: As you grow, your needs and goals may change. Adapt the advice and exercises to fit your evolving journey.

7. **Utilise the Resources**

    - **Additional Resources**: The book may reference additional resources such as books, articles, podcasts, and apps. Explore these to broaden your understanding and find further inspiration.
    - **Community and Support**: Engage with communities, either online or in person, that are focused on personal growth. Sharing your journey with others can provide support and accountability.

8. **Integrate Holistic Practices**

    - **Mind, Body, and Spirit**: Holistic living involves nurturing every aspect of your being. Integrate practices that support your mental, physical, and spiritual health.
    - **Balance**: Strive for balance in all areas of your life. Use the strategies in this book to create harmony and alignment between your goals and daily actions.

9. **Customise Your Journey**

    - **Personalise Your Approach**: Everyone's journey is unique. Customise the advice and practices to fit your personal preferences and lifestyle.
    - **Be Patient and Compassionate**: Personal growth takes time. Be patient with yourself and practise self-compassion throughout this journey.

10. **Stay Committed and Persistent**

    - **Commit to the Process**: Transformation doesn't happen overnight. Stay committed to the process, even when it feels challenging.
    - **Persistence Pays Off**: Remember that persistence is key. The more consistently you apply the principles in this book, the more profound your transformation will be.

Your Journey Begins Here

As you begin this journey, don't wait for the perfect moment to start. The first step is often the hardest, but it's also the most important.

Start with one small change today, and watch how it opens the door to bigger transformations. No matter where you're starting from, you have the power to create lasting change. Every decision you make is a step forward. So, as you dive into the chapters ahead, take that first step with confidence, and know that each small action brings you closer to the life you envision.

"Like a superhero, your power grows not when you avoid challenges, but when you face them head-on."

– Author

A PERSONAL INVITATION

I invite you to dive into this book with an open mind and a willingness to grow. Each chapter is a stepping stone on your path to becoming your best self.

Now, it's time to put your superpowers into action. Start small, with manageable goals that align with your purpose. As you achieve these goals, your confidence will grow, and so will your ability to tackle bigger challenges. Celebrate each victory, no matter how small. Every accomplishment is a foothold on the mountain of success. Rewarding yourself and marking your progress will motivate you to continue the climb.

Understand that failure is part of the process. Even superheroes face defeat. The most important thing is to learn from your mistakes. They are opportunities to grow, learn, and improve. Surround yourself with positive influences. These are your fellow champions – the ones who support, believe in, and cheer you on. They can help you stay on the path and overcome obstacles.

Sometimes, you may feel overwhelmed. When that happens, remember that even superheroes need to recharge. Take time for self-care and relaxation. A rested hero is a powerful hero. Don't compare yourself to others. Your journey is your own, unique and special, just like your superpowers. You're not competing with anyone else; you're striving to be the best version of yourself.

Lastly, never forget the responsibility that comes with being a hero. Your actions impact others. Use your powers to help, inspire, and create positive change. One hero can make a big difference.

Remember, this journey is not a race. It's a continual process of growth, discovery, and transformation.

There's a hero inside all of us, waiting to be unleashed. Believe in yourself, and nothing will be impossible for you.

Let's begin this journey together.

"Unlocking your potential isn't about changing who you are—it's about becoming more of who you were meant to be."

– Author

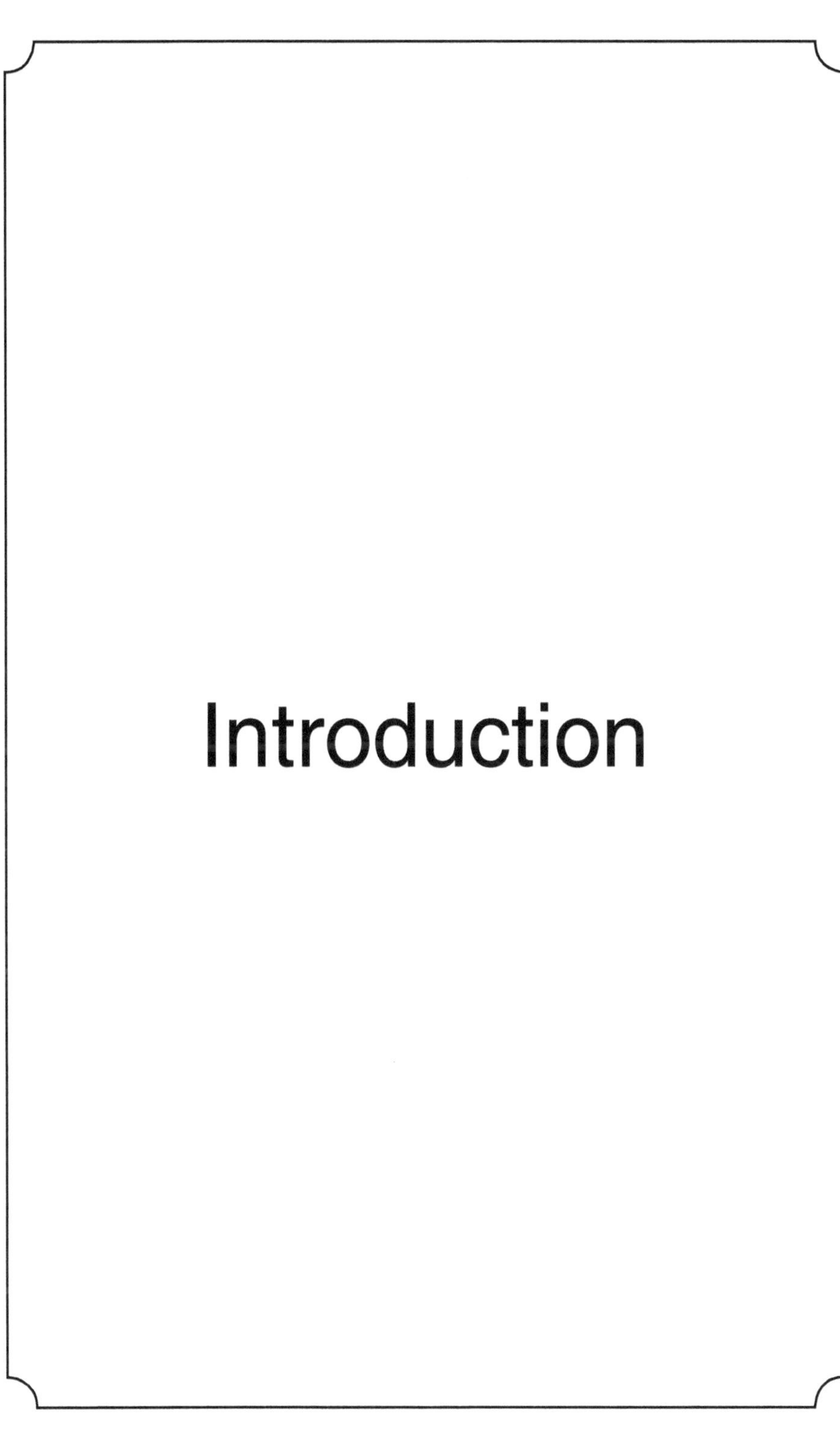

Introduction

Chapter 01

THE JOURNEY TO ABUNDANCE

"Whatever you hold in your mind on a consistent basis is exactly what you will experience in your life."

– Tony Robbins

The Power of Possibility: Nothing is Impossible

The central message of this book is simple yet powerful: nothing is impossible. Whatever your dreams and aspirations, you have the power to achieve them. It all begins with belief—belief in yourself, in your abilities, and in the steps you take to move toward your goals. This book is your guide to making those dreams a reality, offering practical advice, inspiring stories, and actionable steps to support you on your journey. The most powerful tool you have at your disposal is your mind.

"Belief is often the first, and sometimes hardest, hurdle to overcome. Without it, our efforts can feel empty and directionless. But when you believe in yourself, you turn potential into action."

Why Holistic Living Matters

In today's fast-paced world, many of us feel overwhelmed, disconnected, and stuck. We chase success, happiness, and health, often neglecting the very aspects of life that help us achieve these goals.

Often, we focus so intensely on one aspect of our lives—like our careers or business—that we neglect the mental or emotional support we need. Holistic living offers a balanced approach to well-being by nurturing every aspect of your being—physical, mental, emotional, and spiritual. By adopting this approach, you unleash your full potential and create harmony in your life. This balance not only helps you thrive but equips you to navigate life's challenges with resilience and strength.

The Power of Self-Reliance

In the world of films, comics, and stories, superheroes seem to possess extraordinary powers, always arriving at the perfect moment to save the day. But in real life, no one is coming to save us from the challenges we face. When we feel overwhelmed, it's natural to wish for a savior. Yet the truth is that we possess the power to be our own heroes.

This book isn't about waiting for someone to rescue you. It's about recognizing that you have the strength, courage, and resilience to face life's challenges head-on. You already possess the tools to overcome adversity. This book will show you how to harness those internal powers.

"A hero is an ordinary individual who finds the strength to persevere and endure in spite of overwhelming obstacles."

– Christopher Reeve

The Turning Point: Realising No Superhero is Coming

There was a pivotal moment in my life when I faced a seemingly insurmountable challenge. I felt overwhelmed and found myself wishing for someone to come and save me. It was then that I realised no one was coming. I had to become my own superhero.

At first, the idea of relying only on myself was terrifying. I was filled with doubt—'What if I'm not strong enough? What if I fail?' But facing those fears was the very thing that started my transformation. It marked the beginning of my journey toward self-reliance and holistic living.

When we face challenges, it's natural to wish for an external savior. However, true strength comes from understanding that we are our own saviors. This book will equip you with the tools and mindset needed to unlock your inner superhero and overcome life's challenges.

"You don't need superhuman abilities to change your life—just the willingness to take one small, intentional step every day."

– Author

My Journey to Holistic Living

Years ago, I found myself stuck, overworked, and disconnected from my purpose. Despite chasing success, happiness, and financial security, I felt drained. Persistent health issues and overwhelming stress began to impact my work, relationships, and well-being. At first, I hoped for an easy fix—someone or something to rescue me from my struggles. But nothing happened. It was only when I accepted responsibility for my situation and took control that things began to change.

I realised that to truly thrive, I had to make changes across all areas of my life—physical, mental, emotional, and spiritual. I created a comprehensive plan to improve both my physical and mental health. This involved setting realistic health goals, adopting a balanced diet, incorporating exercise, and practicing mindfulness. With professional help and consistent effort, I began to see improvements. This experience taught me the importance of self-reliance, perseverance, and taking control of my life. Slowly, holistic practices became a core part of my routine, and my life was transformed.

The Power of Holistic Living

Holistic living is not about making radical, overnight changes. It's about making small, consistent improvements across all areas of your life. This approach helps you nurture the interconnected aspects of your well-being.

By practicing small, intentional habits daily, you will create a profound transformation over time.

It's easy to get impatient, expecting results overnight. But holistic living is about making small, sustainable changes over time. Be patient with yourself and trust that these daily habits will lead to profound transformations

"That person who helps others simply because it should or must be done, and because it is the right thing to do, is indeed, without a doubt, a real superhero."

– Stan Lee

Practical Example: Health and Fitness

Improving your physical health is a great example of how small, consistent actions lead to big results. When I decided to improve my fitness, I didn't jump into extreme exercise routines. I started with simple, manageable steps—short daily walks, healthier meals, and gradually increasing my activity level. Over time, these small changes led to major improvements in my health. This approach works in any area of life.

Not only did my physical health improve, but I also noticed mental benefits—more energy, clearer thoughts, and a growing sense of accomplishment. The mind and body truly are connected. Focus on small, consistent actions, and the results will follow.

Ask Yourself

1. What areas of your life do you feel need change?
2. What small steps can you take today to start your transformation?
3. How can you build resilience and self-reliance in your daily life?

"The journey to abundance isn't about perfection; it's about progress, resilience, and the belief that each step matters."

– Author

Final Thoughts

In this book, you'll discover the incredible power within you. Through practical steps and holistic practices, you'll learn how to unlock your full potential and become your own superhero. Embrace the journey, and remember, you have the power to transform your life.

Next, we'll dive into *The Power of Mindset*, where you'll learn how your thoughts and beliefs shape your reality—and how to harness that power to unlock greatness!

Section 1

Mindset and Mental Health

Chapter 02

THE POWER OF MINDSET

"Whether you think you can, or you think you can't – you're right."

– Henry Ford

The Power of Thoughts: Mindset Shapes Reality

Our thoughts shape the way we perceive and experience the world around us. They influence our actions, decisions, and ultimately the outcomes we achieve. The quality of our thoughts determines whether we see opportunities or obstacles, success or failure, possibilities or limitations. The power of mindset lies in how it transforms our potential—by adopting a positive and growth-oriented mindset, we can unlock our fullest capabilities.

This chapter explores the immense power of mindset and how it can change your reality. It will provide you with tools and techniques to harness this power and help you create a more fulfilling, successful life.

Changing your mindset isn't always easy. We often hold onto limiting beliefs out of habit or fear, but recognizing them is the first step to breaking free. Like any new habit, building a positive mindset takes time and practice, but the rewards are transformative

"Your thoughts are the architects of your reality. Build wisely, and you'll create the life you've always envisioned."

– Author

The Science Behind Mindset

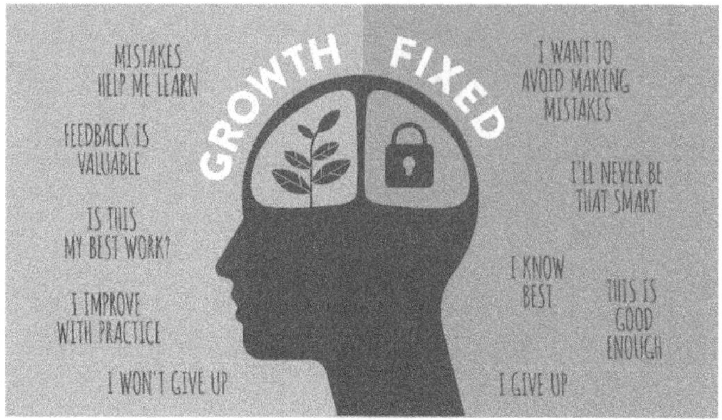

Psychological research strongly supports the idea that our mindset plays a critical role in our success and overall well-being. Dr. Carol S. Dweck, in her groundbreaking book *Mindset: The New Psychology of Success*, identifies two key types of mindsets: the **fixed mindset** and the **growth mindset**.

- **Fixed Mindset**: People with a fixed mindset believe that their abilities, intelligence, and talents are static and unchangeable. They tend to avoid challenges, fear failure, and give up easily when faced with obstacles.
- **Growth Mindset**: On the other hand, individuals with a growth mindset believe that their abilities can be developed through effort, learning, and perseverance. They embrace challenges, learn from feedback, and view failure as an opportunity to grow.

Adopting a growth mindset can lead to greater motivation, resilience, and achievement, whether in your career, relationships, or personal goals.

"A fixed mindset traps you in today's limits, while a growth mindset opens the door to tomorrow's possibilities."

– Author

Inspiring Story: Arunima Sinha – Conquering Everest

One of the most powerful examples of the impact of mindset is the story of **Arunima Sinha**. Arunima was a national-level volleyball player in India when a tragic incident changed her life. In 2011, she was pushed off a moving train during a robbery attempt. She survived the fall but lost one of her legs as a result of the accident.

While most people would have been defeated by such a life-altering event, Arunima's mindset was different. Instead of succumbing to despair, she set herself an unimaginable goal: to climb **Mount Everest**—the highest peak in the world.

Despite the immense physical and emotional challenges, Arunima trained tirelessly, both mentally and physically. In 2013, she became the world's first female amputee to climb Mount Everest.

At her lowest point, Arunima could have easily succumbed to despair. But instead, she made a conscious decision to challenge herself beyond what seemed possible. Each step toward Everest was not just a physical challenge, but a testament to her unshakable belief in her ability to overcome.

Her story is a testament to the power of positive thinking, resilience, and a growth mindset. She teaches us that no challenge is too great when you believe in yourself and your ability to grow through adversity.

Ask Yourself: *If Arunima could climb Mount Everest despite losing her leg, what challenge in your life can you overcome with the right mindset?*

The Transformative Power of Positive Thinking

Your mindset is your superpower. Like superheroes who believe in their ability to overcome any obstacle, adopting a positive mindset can transform your life. Norman Vincent Peale, in *The Power of Positive Thinking*, highlights how a positive mindset helps you face difficulties, increase confidence, and develop inner strength. When you fill your mind with positive, empowering thoughts, you build a foundation for success.

When you think positively:

- You focus on solutions, not problems.
- You approach challenges with confidence.
- You cultivate resilience in the face of setbacks.

Negativity, on the other hand, can become a self-fulfilling prophecy. When we focus on what could go wrong, we limit our potential and may even fail to take the steps needed to move forward.

Personal Story: The Day the World Stopped due to Covid 19

It feels like just yesterday, the vividness of that day remains so clear in my memory. It was March 2020, and my family and I sat glued to the television, watching in disbelief as Prime Minister Narendra Modi declared a nationwide 21-day lockdown. The entire country was coming to a halt, and though we had seen it coming, as the rest of the world slowly shut down, the finality of it still hit hard. The world, as we knew it, had changed.

I was only just beginning to adjust to this new reality when my phone rang. It was the Vice President of Logistics from one of the major FMCG companies I was working with. My logistics company had been providing domestic transportation services to large FMCG and pharmaceutical firms, but now, everything seemed uncertain. The voice on the other end was serious. He explained that there was an urgent consignment of handwash and disinfectants that needed to be delivered to government hospitals across the country. The importance of the request was undeniable, but I found myself thinking of the barriers – curfews on the roads, lockdown restrictions, and the fact that my team, like the rest of the country, was stuck at home.

"I don't think it's possible to mobilize trucks," I responded. "Most of the drivers have already left for their villages, fearing the worst, and my team is also unable to leave their homes." There was a moment of silence, and then came the question that stayed with me: *"Is there at least something you can do?"*

It was in that moment that something clicked inside me. My client's voice wasn't just making a business request; I could hear the urgency, the desire to help people in need during an unprecedented crisis. While every voice inside my head pointed to the challenges, another voice emerged—the one that focused on possibilities. Instead of fixating on the obstacles, I began asking myself, *"What can I do in this situation?"*

I quickly contacted my team, and we worked together to trace the locations of our trucks and drivers. Understandably, they were hesitant to return to work. After all, those were terrifying times. There was fear in the air—fear of the virus, fear for their families, fear of the unknown. But I assured them we would practice the highest levels of safety and sanitation. Slowly, with a collective effort, we began mobilizing a few trucks. Using the permissions from the District Magistrate, which we secured with the help of my client, we slowly started moving.

A couple of days into the operation, I started receiving dozens of phone calls. This time, it was pharmaceutical companies that needed to supply essential medicines to hospitals. Before long, we found ourselves not only delivering disinfectants but also ensuring that life-saving medicines reached where they were needed most.

Every day presented a new challenge. How could we mobilize the team safely from their homes to the warehouses? How could we ensure that truck drivers, many of whom were stranded on highways with no open food outlets, were taken care of? How could we secure spare parts for broken-down trucks or find funds to keep the operations running smoothly when businesses were halting?

Yet, for every challenge, we found a solution. We stopped thinking about what wasn't possible and started focusing on what could be done. Slowly, we restarted our entire logistics infrastructure, ensuring that essential goods reached those who needed them most. What began as an impossible task turned into a mission that not only brought our operations back to life but also gave us a sense of purpose.

The lockdown that began as a 21-day shutdown stretched into months—four long months of uncertainty. But as I look back on those days, I realise that what we achieved could never have been possible without the unwavering commitment of my team and the support of our clients. What truly made the difference was a shift in mindset. That pivotal moment when I asked myself, *"What can I do in this situation?"* became the driving force that allowed us to move forward in the face of uncertainty.

The power of positive thinking is a force beyond measure. It turns obstacles into opportunities and transforms fear into action. My experience during the pandemic lockdown reinforced this truth: When you shift your focus from what you can't do to what you *can* do, solutions begin to appear, and the impossible starts to seem possible.

You, too, have the power to reshape your mindset in moments of crisis. Challenges will always arise, and fear will always try to hold you back. But by focusing on the positive—by asking yourself what you can control, what you can contribute—you unlock the potential to overcome even the most daunting circumstances. It's not about being unrealistic; it's about realizing that within every challenge lies an opportunity to grow, to innovate, and to rise above.

The day the world stopped, I discovered that the only thing more powerful than the challenges before me was my mindset. And that, I believe, is a power we all have within us.

"The pessimist sees difficulty in every opportunity. The optimist sees opportunity in every difficulty."

– Winston Churchill

How to Cultivate a Positive Mindset

Here are a few practical techniques to cultivate a growth-oriented, positive mindset:

1. **Visualisation**: Picture yourself achieving your goals. Elite athletes often use this technique to prepare mentally for competition. Spend a few minutes each day visualising your success and how it feels to achieve your dreams.
2. **Affirmations**: Use daily affirmations to reinforce positive beliefs. Say statements like "I am capable," "I will succeed," or "I have the strength to overcome any obstacle." Over time, affirmations help rewire your brain for success.
3. **Challenge Negative Thoughts**: Whenever a negative thought arises, ask yourself, "Is this true?" Often, negative thoughts are based on fear or insecurity rather than facts. Replace them with positive, empowering thoughts.
4. **Surround Yourself with Positivity**: The people you spend time with influence your mindset. Build a community of positive, supportive individuals who inspire and uplift you. Limit exposure to negativity, whether from people or media.

Be patient with yourself during this process. Building a positive mindset doesn't happen overnight, and setbacks are part of the journey. Celebrate small victories, and know that every effort you make strengthens your new mindset.

Ask Yourself

1. How do you usually respond to challenges? Do you avoid them or embrace them as opportunities to grow?
2. Can you identify any limiting beliefs that hold you back? What positive beliefs can you adopt instead?
3. How can you apply the story of Arunima Sinha to your own life?

Time to Take Action

1. **Mindset Journal**: Start a mindset journal. Write down one challenge you faced and how your mindset influenced your response. Reflect on whether you approached it with a fixed or growth mindset.

Example:

I set a fitness goal to lose weight, and at first, I made great progress, losing a few kilos. But recently, my weight has plateaued, and I'm no longer seeing the same results. My fixed mindset told me, "Maybe this is as far as I can go." After reflecting, I realised that many people experience plateaus in their fitness journey. By adopting a growth mindset, I reminded myself, "I can overcome this by tweaking my routine and being patient." I adjusted my diet and exercise plan, and this renewed sense of control helped me stay motivated to continue toward my goal.

2. **Visualisation Exercise**: Spend five minutes each morning visualising yourself achieving one of your major goals. Imagine it in detail—how you'll feel, what you'll experience, and what success looks like.

   Example:

   I'm working towards saving enough money to buy my first home. Each morning, I visualize myself walking through the door of my new house, feeling the sense of security and accomplishment. I imagine how I'll decorate it and the joy of having a place to call my own. This vision keeps me on track with my financial goals and reminds me that each small saving decision brings me closer to this reality.

Final Thoughts

Your mindset shapes your reality. By adopting a growth mindset, like Arunima Sinha did, you can turn obstacles into stepping stones and limitations into opportunities for growth. Mindset is a superpower that every one of us possesses, and with the right attitude, there's no limit to what you can achieve.

Chapter 03

THE POWER OF REFLECTION, SELF-AWARENESS AND HEALING

"Knowing yourself is the beginning of all wisdom."

– Aristotle

The Role of Reflection and Self-Awareness in Personal Growth

Self-awareness and reflection are at the heart of personal development. They allow us to pause, look inward, and understand our thoughts, behaviors, and motivations. Like superheroes who regularly evaluate their actions and experiences to sharpen their abilities, reflection helps us learn from the past, grow emotionally, and gain greater clarity about our path.

Developing self-awareness enables you to:

- Understand your strengths and weaknesses
- Make better decisions
- Cultivate emotional intelligence
- Live a more mindful and fulfilling life

Self-awareness can feel uncomfortable at times, especially when it forces us to face parts of ourselves that we've avoided. But it's through this discomfort that true growth happens. Embrace the process, knowing that every insight brings you closer to becoming your best self.

In this chapter, we will explore how reflection, self-awareness, and healing from past wounds are interconnected and essential to becoming your best self.

"Self-awareness is the key that unlocks the door to growth, and healing is the path that leads you through it."

– Author

The Science Behind Reflection and Self-Awareness

Research has consistently shown the powerful benefits of reflection and self-awareness. In a study published in the *Journal of Personality and Social Psychology*, individuals who regularly engage in self-reflection report higher levels of emotional intelligence, better decision-making skills, and greater overall well-being.

Similarly, a study by the *Harvard Business Review* highlights that self-aware individuals—especially leaders—tend to have better relationships, improved empathy, and more effective communication. Regular reflection also helps identify areas of improvement, giving you the tools to evolve and grow.

Real-Life Inspiration: The Story of Oprah Winfrey

One of the most iconic examples of how reflection and healing can transform lives is the story of **Oprah Winfrey**. Today, Oprah is a global media mogul, but her journey was filled with trauma, abuse, and immense hardships. Born into poverty, Oprah faced significant challenges growing up, including sexual abuse and emotional neglect.

Rather than allowing her painful past to define her future, Oprah embraced the power of self-reflection. She spent years processing her emotions, healing from her traumas, and reframing her narrative. Oprah didn't just heal—she thrived, becoming a beacon of inspiration for millions. Her ability to reflect on her experiences, learn from them, and use them as fuel for growth showcases the transformative power of self-awareness and healing.

Ask Yourself: *If Oprah can overcome such adversity and create a life of success and fulfillment, what lessons from your past can you use to fuel your own growth?*

Healing from the Past: The Path to Emotional Freedom

To truly unlock your inner superhero, you must heal from the past. Every person carries wounds—whether they stem from childhood experiences, broken relationships, or personal failures. These unprocessed emotions can weigh us down, creating mental and emotional barriers that prevent us from moving forward.

Healing isn't a straight line—it's a journey full of ups and downs. Some days you'll feel lighter and more at peace, while others will bring emotional challenges. The key is to remain patient and compassionate with yourself during the process."

Healing from the past doesn't mean forgetting or dismissing your experiences. It means acknowledging them, processing the emotions tied to them, and letting go of the pain that holds you back.

"You cannot change what happened, but you can change how it defines you. Healing is the power to rewrite your story."

– Author

Practical Example: Letting Go in Professional Life

Consider the story of Steve Jobs. After being ousted from Apple, the company he co-founded, Jobs could have easily harboured resentment or anger. Instead, he chose to let go of the bitterness and channel his energy into new creative ventures. This decision led to his founding of NeXT and Pixar, both of which significantly impacted the tech and entertainment industries. Eventually, his journey of letting go and finding inner peace brought him back to Apple, where he revolutionized the company and introduced some of the world's most iconic products, like the iPhone and iPad.

Jobs' story demonstrates that letting go of past failures can lead to future success and fulfilment. His ability to embrace new opportunities and focus on inner peace was critical to his remarkable career.

Ask Yourself: *Is there a professional failure or setback in your life that you need to let go of to create space for new opportunities?*

The Power of Forgiveness

One of the most powerful tools in healing is forgiveness—both of others and yourself. Forgiveness doesn't mean condoning wrong actions. Instead, it's about freeing yourself from the emotional burden of resentment and pain.

Consider the story of **Immaculée Ilibagiza**, a survivor of the Rwandan genocide. During the genocide, Immaculée hid in a small bathroom for 91 days with seven other women, fearing for her life. She later discovered that her entire family, except for one brother, had been killed. Despite the horror and trauma, Immaculée found peace through forgiveness. She forgave the people who killed her family and dedicated her life to spreading messages of forgiveness, love, and healing.

Her story reminds us that even in the face of unimaginable pain, healing is possible through forgiveness.

Ask Yourself: *Is there someone in your life—perhaps even yourself—that you need to forgive in order to heal and move forward?*

How to Forgive When Someone Does Not Deserve Forgiveness: My Personal Journey

Forgiveness can feel impossible when someone has deeply wronged you, especially when they don't seem to deserve it. Holding onto that anger, however, doesn't just hurt them—it holds *you* captive. Over the years, I held grudges and even hatred towards people who had wronged me. "Hatred" is a strong word, but sometimes, it feels justified when someone has been intentionally cruel. It can feel like harboring that resentment is a way of keeping the person accountable, as if withholding forgiveness makes them pay for their wrongs.

I used to believe that, too. But then one day, I experienced a shift. It happened while watching a seemingly ordinary movie—*Bachna Ae Haseeno*—with my family. In the movie, Ranbir Kapoor's character abandons Bipasha Basu's character on the day of their wedding, leaving her alone on the courthouse steps. Her heart is broken, and she carries deep resentment toward him for years, becoming hardened by the bitterness.

Much later, after realizing the gravity of his mistake, Ranbir's character returns, seeking forgiveness. He tries repeatedly to apologize, but she insists that what he did was unforgivable. And who could blame her? He didn't deserve forgiveness. But in the end, something remarkable happens: Bipasha chooses to forgive him—not because he earned it, but because she wanted to free herself from the weight of her past. She didn't want her bitterness to define her anymore.

That moment hit me hard, as if it were an answer to my own struggles. I realised I had been clinging to my anger, using it as a shield, but in doing so, I was only hurting myself. Forgiveness wasn't about letting those people off the hook for their cruelty—it was about freeing *myself* from the hold they still had over me.

The Turning Point: Choosing Peace

In that moment, watching Bipasha's character let go of her hatred, I felt something unlock inside me. It was as if the film was mirroring my own struggles. I had always believed that forgiveness was conditional—that the person had to apologize, change, or somehow make amends before they deserved to be forgiven. But what if they never did? Should I stay chained to the past, waiting for an apology that might never come?

The answer was clear: no. That day I forgave everyone who had wronged me, not for their sake, but for my own. I realised that by holding onto hatred, I was giving power to those who had hurt me. They didn't deserve that power. I did.

The Misconception About Forgiveness

One of the greatest misconceptions about forgiveness is that it's for the other person—that somehow, they need to deserve it. But forgiveness isn't a gift you give them—it's a gift you give yourself. By holding onto grudges, you're allowing the person who hurt you to continue affecting your life. The truth is, forgiveness is about reclaiming your peace.

There's power in the realization that you don't need the other person to apologize or even change for you to forgive them. You forgive because *you* deserve peace. When you harbor hatred or resentment, it festers inside you, impacting your emotional, mental, and even physical well-being. Forgiveness allows you to let go of that negativity, not because the person deserves it, but because *you* deserve to move forward.

Forgiveness as Freedom

Forgiving someone who doesn't deserve it doesn't mean you condone their actions. It doesn't mean you forget what they did or let them back into your life. Instead, it's about accepting that their actions were wrong, but you're choosing to release the hold those actions have on you. Forgiveness is about creating emotional space for peace, healing, and growth.

In the end, forgiveness is not about making the other person feel better—it's about lightening your own emotional burden. Forgiveness doesn't mean forgetting. It means accepting what happened, learning from it, and moving on without letting it define you. It's about saying, "You hurt me, but I will not let that pain control me anymore."

"Forgiveness is not about forgetting—it's about freeing yourself to live fully in the present."

– Author

Key Components of Reflection, Self-Awareness, and Healing

1. **Regular Reflection**: Set aside time to reflect on your thoughts, actions, and experiences. Reflection allows you to learn from both successes and failures, providing insights for future growth.

2. **Seeking Feedback**: Self-awareness isn't just about internal reflection. Seeking feedback from trusted individuals offers valuable external perspectives and helps you understand how others perceive you.
3. **Self-Compassion**: Treat yourself with kindness and understanding. Acknowledge that everyone makes mistakes and experiences pain. Practicing self-compassion fosters healing and encourages self-growth.
4. **Creating New Narratives**: Reframe your past experiences as lessons that have strengthened you. Rather than seeing yourself as a victim, view yourself as a resilient survivor who has gained valuable insights through adversity.

Ask Yourself

1. What past experiences or unresolved emotions are holding you back from living your best life?
2. How do you typically process difficult emotions? Do you avoid them or face them head-on?
3. What steps can you take to increase your self-awareness and begin the process of healing from your past?

Time to Take Action

1. **Forgiveness Letter**: Write a letter to someone from your past (or to yourself) expressing forgiveness. You don't need to send it—this exercise is about acknowledging your emotions and releasing any resentment or pain.

   Example:

   Imagine you had a fallout with a close friend years ago because they let you down during a tough time. You've been holding onto that hurt for years, even though life has moved on. In your forgiveness letter, write down exactly how their actions made you feel—express the anger, the sadness, and the betrayal you experienced. Then, shift the tone of your letter to forgiveness:

"I've carried this hurt for a long time, but I now realise that holding onto it is only weighing me down. I forgive you for not being there, and I'm choosing to release this pain for my own peace."

2. **Creative Expression**: Use creative outlets such as drawing, painting, or music to process your emotions related to past experiences. Creativity is a powerful way to release pent-up feelings and foster healing.

   Example:

   Let's say you experienced a challenging breakup that left you emotionally drained. Instead of just talking about your pain, try painting. You may not know exactly what to paint, but let your emotions guide you—use colours that represent your feelings, whether it's the darkness of blue and black to symbolize grief or the brightness of yellow to reflect moments of peace. The act of painting allows you to express what words might not capture. As you finish your piece, you might notice that some of the weight you've been carrying has started to lift, allowing space for self-awareness and healing.

   Creativity in this form becomes a dialogue between your emotions and your healing process.

Final Thoughts

Reflection, self-awareness, and healing from the past are all essential steps in unlocking your inner superhero. By regularly reflecting on your experiences, cultivating self-awareness, and taking the time to heal from emotional wounds, you free yourself from the burdens of the past and move forward with clarity and strength.

The journey toward self-awareness and healing is ongoing. Embrace the process, and remember that every step, no matter how small, is progress. By looking inward, you'll gain the wisdom and resilience to overcome any challenge that comes your way. Let this be the chapter that empowers you to reflect, heal, and transform into the superhero you are destined to become.

Section 2

Physical Health and Wellness

Chapter 04

PHYSICAL HEALTH – THE FOUNDATION OF A FULFILLING LIFE

"Take care of your body. It's the only place you have to live."

– Jim Rohn

The Importance of Physical Health

When you think of the term "life partner," most people immediately picture their spouse or significant other—someone with whom they share their life and future. For some, the notion extends to family members, like parents or children, or perhaps a lifelong friend. But how often do you consider your body to be your truest life partner? From your first breath to your last, it is your body that accompanies you through every experience, every emotion, and every milestone.

Unlike any other relationship, your bond with your body is unbreakable. It is with you in times of joy and sorrow, success and failure, health and illness. Yet, we often neglect this most fundamental of relationships. We push our bodies beyond their limits, ignore warning signs, and fail to give them the care they deserve. However, nurturing this relationship can bring you strength, vitality, and resilience.

Embracing your body as your true life partner is a transformative shift in mindset. When you view your body as your closest ally, you'll want to nurture it, respect it, and prioritize its well-being. This is the foundation of a fulfilling life because when your body thrives, so do you.

When you treat your body as your life partner, you'll notice the ripple effects—improved focus at work, deeper connections with loved ones, and a stronger sense of overall well-being. Taking care of your body is the key to showing up fully in every area of life.

"Your body is not just a vessel—it's your lifelong partner. Nurture it, and it will carry you toward your fullest potential."

– Author

Be Your Own Superhero: Prioritizing Physical Health

Superheroes are defined by their resilience, strength, and ability to face challenges head-on. Similarly, to be your own superhero, you must prioritize your physical health. Physical fitness is the cornerstone of overall well-being and plays a crucial role in your mental and emotional health as well. When your body is healthy, your mind is clearer, your emotions more balanced, and your energy more vibrant.

Taking care of your body empowers you to show up as your best self every day. Whether you're facing professional challenges, personal growth, or simply the demands of daily life, your physical health is your greatest asset.

Just as superheroes train to enhance their abilities, taking care of your body builds discipline and resilience in all areas of life. Every workout, healthy meal, and good night's sleep is an investment in your physical, mental, and emotional strength.

The Connection Between Physical Health and Holistic Living

Holistic living is about nurturing every aspect of your being—your mind, body, and spirit. Each of these elements is interconnected, and physical health plays a central role in supporting the other two. When your body is functioning optimally, it has a direct impact on your mental clarity, emotional resilience, and overall quality of life. Conversely, when you neglect your physical health, it can lead to stress, anxiety, and a lack of motivation.

Real-Life Example: Neeraj's Wake-Up Call

Consider the story of Neeraj, a friend of mine. One morning, I received an early phone call from him, and the anxiety in his voice was palpable. He explained that during the night, he had woken up with a terrifying sensation—he felt like he was choking, struggling for air as if someone was squeezing his neck. Panicked, he consulted a doctor later that morning, who diagnosed him with sleep apnea, caused by the fat pressing against his airway due to his excess weight.

Years of indulging in unhealthy eating, late-night parties, and a sedentary lifestyle had caught up with him. Neeraj was forced to confront the hard truth: his neglect of his physical health had serious consequences. That experience became his wake-up call. Determined to turn things around, Neeraj completely transformed his lifestyle. He adopted a balanced diet, incorporated regular exercise, reduced alcohol consumption, and prioritised sleep. Slowly, but surely, Neeraj started to regain control of his health and well-being, realizing that his body was his most valuable life partner.

As Neeraj regained control of his physical health, he noticed not just physical improvements, but also mental clarity and emotional resilience. By prioritizing his body, he found the energy and focus to thrive in other areas of his life.

This experience highlights an essential truth: without prioritizing your physical health, you risk not only your physical well-being but also your overall quality of life.

Ask Yourself: *If Neeraj could make such significant changes in his life despite years of unhealthy habits, what is stopping you from taking control of your own health today?*

Key Components of Physical Health

1. **Nutrition**: A balanced diet is essential for fueling your body with the nutrients it needs to function optimally. Whole, nutrient-dense foods—

like fruits, vegetables, lean proteins, and whole grains—provide the foundation for good health. Avoid processed foods, excessive sugar, and unhealthy fats, which can lead to chronic illness and reduced vitality.

2. **Exercise**: Regular physical activity is vital for maintaining muscle strength, cardiovascular health, and mental clarity. Aim for at least 150 minutes of moderate aerobic exercise or 75 minutes of vigorous activity per week. Incorporate strength training and flexibility exercises for overall fitness.
3. **Sleep**: Quality sleep is critical for physical recovery, cognitive function, and emotional balance. Adults should aim for 7-9 hours of sleep each night. Developing a consistent sleep routine and creating a restful sleep environment can improve the quality of your sleep.
4. **Hydration**: Staying hydrated supports digestion, circulation, and energy levels. It's recommended to drink at least eight glasses of water daily, but this amount may vary based on your level of physical activity and climate.
5. **Stress Management**: Chronic stress takes a toll on both physical and mental health. Incorporating stress-relief practices, such as mindfulness, meditation, yoga, or deep breathing exercises, into your daily routine can significantly improve your overall well-being.

It's not about perfection—it's about consistency. Small, steady improvements in your diet, exercise routine, and sleep habits will lead to big results over time. Your body responds to consistency, so don't give up after a few setbacks

"Let food be thy medicine and medicine be thy food."

– Hippocrates

Ask Yourself

1. What current habits are negatively affecting your physical health?
2. What small, manageable changes can you make to improve your diet, exercise routine, sleep, and hydration?

3. How can you incorporate stress management practices into your daily life to support your overall well-being?

Time to Take Action

1. **Health Assessment**: Take a personal inventory of your current health habits in the areas of nutrition, exercise, sleep, hydration, and stress management. Identify which areas need improvement and why.

   Example:

   As I took stock of my current habits, I realised that while I'm fairly active, my diet could use improvement. I tend to skip breakfast and grab fast food for lunch because of my busy schedule. As a result, I often feel sluggish in the afternoons and lack energy. I also noticed that I've been averaging only 5-6 hours of sleep per night, which leaves me feeling drained. My hydration is decent, but stress management is another area I could improve—I tend to let work stress build up without having a proper outlet.

2. **Goal Setting (Using SMART Criteria)**

   Exercise: Using the SMART criteria (Specific, Measurable, Achievable, Relevant, Time-bound), write down specific goals for each aspect of your physical health.

   Example:

   I will walk for 30 minutes, three times a week, for the next month.

Final Thoughts

Prioritizing your physical health is one of the most powerful steps you can take toward living a fulfilling life. By nurturing your body through proper nutrition, regular exercise, adequate sleep, hydration, and stress management, you are not only improving your physical health but also your emotional and mental well-being.

Like Neeraj, you have the ability to transform your health and unlock your inner superhero. It begins with small, intentional actions that lead to lasting change. Remember, your body is your true life partner, and taking care of it is the foundation for achieving your fullest potential.

Chapter 05

EMBRACING WELLNESS – PHYSICAL, MENTAL, AND EMOTIONAL HEALTH

"The greatest medicine of all is teaching people how not to need it."

– Hippocrates

The Holistic Approach to Wellness

Wellness is not just the absence of illness; it is a state of complete physical, mental, and emotional well-being. Like superheroes who need their strength, focus, and emotional resilience to combat villains, we too must strengthen all aspects of ourselves to thrive in life.

A holistic approach to wellness emphasises the importance of balancing physical, mental, and emotional health. Achieving wellness in just one area is not enough for a fulfilling life; it's the integration of all three that provides the foundation for lasting health and happiness. By nurturing every aspect of your well-being, you not only enhance your quality of life but also cultivate the resilience and energy needed to meet life's challenges.

Be Your Own Superhero: Embracing Holistic Wellness

To be your own superhero, it's essential to embrace the full spectrum of wellness: mind, body, and spirit. Superheroes aren't only physically strong; they are emotionally intelligent and mentally sharp. Similarly, by prioritizing holistic wellness, you can build the resilience and energy required to thrive in every aspect of your life.

We often focus so much on physical fitness that we overlook our emotional well-being or mental health. But just like a superhero can't rely on strength alone, we too must strengthen every part of ourselves to live a balanced and fulfilling life."

The Science Behind Holistic Wellness

Numerous studies have confirmed that holistic wellness improves overall health outcomes. Research published in *The Lancet* found that individuals who integrate physical, mental, and emotional wellness practices into their routines are not only healthier but also experience longer, more fulfilling lives. Another study in the *American Journal of Public Health* showed that those who prioritize mental and emotional well-being alongside physical health are significantly less likely to develop chronic conditions such as cardiovascular disease or diabetes. The evidence is clear: nurturing all three aspects of wellness creates lasting, positive effects on both body and mind.

Real-Life Example: Novak Djokovic's Wellness Transformation

A compelling example of holistic wellness in action comes from tennis legend **Novak Djokovic**. In the early stages of his career, Djokovic struggled with physical stamina, frequently retiring from matches due to fatigue. His mental clarity often wavered under pressure, and emotionally, he found it difficult to manage his frustrations.

Everything changed when Djokovic began focusing on holistic wellness. He adopted a gluten-free diet after discovering sensitivities that were affecting his performance. Physically, he committed to yoga and mindful stretching routines that improved his flexibility and recovery. Mentally, he integrated mindfulness and visualization techniques to enhance focus and resilience. Emotionally, Djokovic worked on managing his responses to stress, using meditation and breathing exercises to maintain calm during high-stakes moments.

This holistic transformation turned Djokovic from a talented but inconsistent player into one of the most dominant athletes in tennis history. His ability to merge physical health, mental sharpness, and emotional balance into his routine is a testament to the power of embracing wellness across all aspects of life.

By strengthening his emotional resilience and mental clarity, Djokovic was able to manage high-pressure situations and recover from setbacks with a calm, focused mindset.

Ask Yourself: *If Djokovic could achieve such remarkable growth by committing to his well-being, what's stopping you from taking a similar approach?*

Key Components of Holistic Wellness

1. **Physical Health**: Physical wellness is the foundation of holistic health. Regular physical activity, balanced nutrition, sleep, and preventive healthcare form the cornerstone. Physical well-being has a profound impact on both mental clarity and emotional stability.
2. **Mental Health**: Mental wellness is essential for cognitive function, emotional stability, and stress management. Mindfulness, mental stimulation, and practices that challenge the brain help maintain mental sharpness and reduce anxiety.
3. **Emotional Health**: Emotional well-being focuses on understanding and managing your emotions, building meaningful relationships, and developing self-compassion. Being emotionally grounded is key to resilience and lasting happiness.

Like Djokovic, integrating practices that strengthen all three areas of wellness leads to improved energy, better focus, and enhanced overall well-being.

The Importance of Emotional Awareness in Wellness

When we talk about wellness, it's easy to focus on the physical aspect while neglecting emotional health. But your emotions play a crucial role in your overall well-being. Being emotionally aware means understanding and accepting your feelings without being controlled by them. Studies show that emotional regulation is closely linked to better physical health outcomes. For example, the *Journal of Psychosomatic Research* published findings showing that individuals who practice emotional awareness are less likely to suffer from stress-related illnesses like high blood pressure and heart disease.

One practice that fosters emotional wellness is **emotional journaling**. By writing about your feelings, whether it's frustration, joy, or uncertainty, you give yourself the space to process emotions and gain clarity. This practice is especially useful in managing stress or anxiety, as it helps to externalize your thoughts rather than internalizing them. In doing so, you create a healthier emotional state and avoid the pitfalls of bottled-up emotions, which can negatively impact your physical health.

When emotions are suppressed, they don't just disappear—they manifest in physical ways, contributing to stress, fatigue, and even illness. Emotional awareness isn't just about feeling better; it's about taking care of your whole self.

"The path to lasting wellness is built one small, mindful step at a time."

– Author

Incorporating Mental Stimulation into Wellness

While exercise and emotional management are often prioritized in wellness routines, mental stimulation is just as important for keeping your brain sharp and adaptable. Engaging in mentally challenging activities, like learning a new language, solving puzzles, or even exploring creative pursuits like painting or playing a musical instrument, can strengthen neural connections.

One simple way to start incorporating mental stimulation into your daily life is through "mental sprints"—short, intense bursts of learning or creativity. You might spend 10 minutes a day reading an article outside your field of expertise or challenging yourself to solve a brain teaser. Over time, these short activities can significantly improve cognitive flexibility and problem-solving skills.

"To keep the body in good health is a duty... otherwise we shall not be able to keep our mind strong and clear."

– Lao Tzu

Ask Yourself

1. What aspects of your physical, mental, and emotional health are currently neglected?
2. What small adjustments can you make to your daily life to better integrate wellness across these three areas?
3. How can you incorporate practices like emotional journaling or mental stimulation into your daily routine to improve holistic wellness?

Creating a Wellness Routine That Sticks

Building a wellness routine that balances physical, mental, and emotional health requires commitment but is entirely achievable with small, consistent actions. Here's how to create a sustainable, holistic wellness routine:

Time to Take Action

1. **Start Small**: Begin by making minor adjustments. For example, if you want to improve your physical health, start with 10-minute walks. If mental wellness is your focus, add 5 minutes of meditation or deep breathing daily. Over time, gradually increase these practices.

2. **Celebrate Small Wins**: Wellness is a journey, not a destination. Celebrate the small victories, like hitting a new personal best in a workout or successfully meditating for a week straight. These achievements will motivate you to continue improving.

Remember, wellness is personal. What works for one person may not work for you, and that's okay. Adapt your routine in a way that fits your lifestyle and makes you feel empowered, rather than restricted.

Final Thoughts

Embracing holistic wellness means recognizing that physical health, mental clarity, and emotional resilience are all integral parts of a healthy and fulfilling life. Just as Novak Djokovic transformed his career by addressing his well-being in a holistic manner, you too can unlock your best self by nurturing all aspects of your health. Remember, the journey to wellness is a marathon, not a sprint—small, consistent steps will lead to long-term transformation. Embrace the process, and watch as your life begins to flourish in extraordinary ways.

Chapter 06

BUILDING HEALTHY HABITS

"We are what we repeatedly do. Excellence, then, is not an act, but a habit."

– Aristotle

The Power of Habits

Habits are the invisible architecture of our lives. They shape not only our day-to-day activities but also our long-term successes and failures. In superhero stories, characters like Batman or Wonder Woman don't wake up one day as extraordinary beings—they rely on consistent routines, intense training, and disciplined practices that turn them into heroes capable of saving the world. Similarly, in our own lives, it's our habits that set the foundation for long-lasting health, well-being, and fulfillment.

Your habits are the building blocks of who you are and who you will become. By cultivating healthy habits, you can enhance your physical and mental health, increase productivity, and create a life of purpose and achievement. In this chapter, we will explore the importance of healthy habits and how you can integrate them into your life to unlock your inner superhero.

Just as healthy habits can build the foundation for success, unhealthy habits can slowly chip away at our progress. Recognizing these habits is the first step in reshaping them into behaviors that support your goals.

"Your habits are the invisible threads that weave the fabric of your life. Strengthen them, and you strengthen yourself."

– Author

Be Your Own Superhero: Cultivating Healthy Habits

To be your own superhero, you need to create habits that align with your long-term goals. Healthy habits don't just improve your physical fitness—they shape your mindset, boost your emotional resilience, and help you stay focused on what matters most. The key lies in consistency, intentionality, and starting with manageable steps. Just as superheroes rely on their training and discipline, you too can become your own hero by building the habits that support your well-being.

Just like superheroes aren't born with all their powers fully developed, you don't need to be perfect from day one. The key is to start small, stay consistent, and allow your habits to evolve into a powerful force for transformation.

The Science Behind Building Healthy Habits

Research shows that building and maintaining habits isn't just about willpower. In fact, studies, like those from the *European Journal of Social Psychology*, reveal that it takes an average of **66 days** to form a habit—longer than the traditional belief of 21 days. This underlines the importance of patience and consistency in habit formation. The *American Psychological Association* further highlights that habits contribute to mental resilience, productivity, and overall life satisfaction, making them vital to long-term health and success.

Real-Life Case Study: Serena Williams and Habitual Mastery

Take the example of tennis legend **Serena Williams**. What makes Serena stand apart isn't just her physical ability, but the powerful habits she has cultivated over time. From waking up at the crack of dawn for practice to meticulous attention to nutrition and rest, Serena's habits are a testament to her long-lasting success. Her habit of consistent self-improvement—whether that's practicing her serve for hours or focusing on mental strength through meditation—has led her to win multiple Grand Slam titles.

Serena's success shows that it's not about sudden breakthroughs but the gradual layering of habits over time. These small daily habits, when accumulated, propel you toward excellence. Serena's story is a reminder that greatness doesn't come from sporadic efforts but from sustained, intentional habits.

Ask Yourself: *If she could achieve greatness through daily dedication and persistence, what habits can you start building today to move closer to your own goals?*

Key Components of Building Healthy Habits

1. **Identify Key Habits**: Begin by identifying the habits that will have the greatest positive impact on your life. Whether it's exercising, meditating, or committing to healthier eating, focus on the areas that align with your personal goals and well-being.
2. **Start Small**: The biggest mistake people make when building habits is trying to overhaul everything at once. Start small. If you want to meditate, begin with 5 minutes. If you want to exercise, start with 10-minute walks. These manageable steps lay the groundwork for lasting change.
3. **Consistency Over Intensity**: Habits are less about intensity and more about repetition. It's not about working out for three hours on a Sunday—it's about showing up for 20 minutes each day. The key is consistency, which helps turn behaviors into automatic routines.
4. **Create a System**: James Clear, in his book *Atomic Habits*, emphasises the importance of systems over goals. Instead of only focusing on outcomes, build a system that supports your habits. For example, if you aim to eat healthier, plan and prep your meals in advance so that your environment supports your goal.

5. **Positive Reinforcement**: Acknowledge your wins, no matter how small. Each time you stick to a habit, give yourself credit. This positive reinforcement creates an emotional reward that encourages repetition.

Why Habits Fail and How to Succeed

Many people struggle with maintaining habits because they try to rely solely on willpower. Willpower, as research shows, is a finite resource. When it's drained, people fall back on old routines.

Willpower, like a battery, depletes over time—especially after making countless decisions throughout the day. That's why systems are essential: they take the pressure off willpower by automating your habits and making healthy choices easier.

Instead of relying on willpower alone, try these **actionable strategies**:

- **Environment Design**: Make your environment work for you. If you're trying to build a reading habit, keep books visible and easily accessible. If you want to eat healthier, stock your fridge with nutritious options and limit temptations.
- **Habit Stacking**: This involves attaching a new habit to an existing one. For example, if you already have a morning coffee routine, stack a new habit of journaling or stretching right after. The existing routine acts as a cue for the new habit.
- **Accountability Partners**: Share your goals with someone who can hold you accountable. Whether it's a friend, family member, or colleague, having someone to check in with can boost motivation and consistency.

"Success is not about sudden breakthroughs; it's the quiet discipline of showing up, day after day, until your habits become your superpower."

– Author

Call to Reflection and Action

Building healthy habits is not just about bettering yourself—it's about reshaping your entire approach to life. Reflect on the habits that currently shape your daily routine. Are they propelling you toward your goals or holding you back? The key is to be honest with yourself. You have the power to break free from unhealthy habits and replace them with new ones that align with your best self.

Ask Yourself:

1. What habits are currently influencing your life, and are they positive or negative?
2. What small, manageable habit could you start today that would have a significant impact a year from now?
3. How can you build a system that supports your new habit rather than relying solely on willpower?

Time to Take Action

1. **Habit Identification Exercise**: Write down your current habits across physical, mental, and emotional areas. Categorize them into two columns: "Helpful Habits" and "Harmful Habits." Identify one harmful habit to eliminate and one helpful habit to strengthen over the next 30 days.

2. **System Design**: Pick one habit you want to adopt. Now, design a system around it.

   Example: If your goal is to meditate each morning, lay out your meditation cushion or mat the night before. If you're working on fitness, set out your workout clothes in advance or schedule a workout buddy to join you.

Final Thoughts: Supercharge Your Life with Habits

Healthy habits are the cornerstone of personal transformation. As Serena Williams has shown us, it's not just raw talent but consistent, intentional habits that lead to greatness. You don't need to overhaul your life overnight. Start small. Stay consistent. Track your progress. Over time, these seemingly insignificant daily actions will compound, leading to a life filled with purpose, vitality, and achievement.

As you build your habits, remember that this is a lifelong journey. You'll encounter setbacks, but each day offers a new opportunity to get back on track. You are the superhero of your own story, and by harnessing the power of habits, you can achieve greatness in all aspects of your life.

Section 3

Relationships and Community

Chapter 07

BUILDING AND MAINTAINING MEANINGFUL RELATIONSHIPS

"Surround yourself with only people who are going to lift you higher."

– Oprah Winfrey

Introduction: The Importance of Relationships

Human beings thrive in the company of others. Relationships, whether with family, friends, colleagues, or even strangers, form the backbone of our well-being. Superheroes, too, often have strong allies and relationships that provide emotional support, wisdom, and strength during trying times. Similarly, the relationships we cultivate in our lives profoundly affect our happiness, health, and success.

Meaningful relationships provide more than just companionship—they are a source of resilience, offering emotional support when we're struggling and joy during life's victories. In this chapter, we'll explore the role of healthy relationships in your journey toward unlocking your inner superhero and how these connections help you grow personally and emotionally.

In today's world, it's easy to mistake social media interactions for genuine relationships. While technology helps us stay in touch, meaningful connections require more than likes or comments—they thrive on real, intentional communication.

"The quality of your relationships shapes the quality of your life. Nurture the bonds that bring out the best in you."

– Author

Be Your Own Superhero: Strengthening Your Connections

To embody the strength of your inner superhero, you must cultivate and strengthen the relationships in your life. Meaningful connections provide a support system that can lift you through the ups and downs of life. Like any superhero team, your relationships offer insight, emotional energy, and shared wisdom. However, these bonds require nurturing to flourish. It's not just about having people in your life but about maintaining relationships built on trust, respect, and open communication.

Just as superheroes rely on their allies for strength and guidance, meaningful relationships are a two-way street. By offering support and being open to receiving it, you create stronger, more resilient bonds.

The Science of Relationships and Well-Being

Relationships are not only emotionally fulfilling but have a measurable impact on physical and mental health. According to the *Harvard Study of Adult Development*—one of the longest-running studies on human well-being—good relationships are the single most important factor in living a happier and healthier life.

Key Findings from the Harvard Study:

1. **Quality Over Quantity**: It's the quality, not the number of relationships, that matters most. Deep, supportive connections with a few people improve emotional well-being far more than having numerous shallow connections.
2. **Loneliness is Detrimental**: Loneliness can be as harmful to health as smoking or obesity. People who feel isolated are at greater risk for emotional distress and physical illness.

3. **Close Relationships Protect Our Health**: Warm, supportive relationships can prevent or mitigate mental health issues and physical decline, while conflict-laden relationships are harmful to overall well-being.
4. **The Power of Emotional Support**: Emotional closeness is a more accurate predictor of long-term happiness than fame or wealth.

Studies also show that strong social ties can reduce stress and even extend your lifespan. When you surround yourself with supportive relationships, your body benefits just as much as your mind and heart.

"In meaningful relationships, we find the resilience to face life's challenges and the joy to celebrate life's victories."

– Author

Real-Life Case Study: Maya Angelou and Her Circle of Influence

The great writer and civil rights activist **Maya Angelou** exemplifies the importance of meaningful relationships. Despite facing incredible hardship in her early life, Angelou's strength and perseverance were amplified by the supportive people around her. She forged deep connections with influential figures like James Baldwin, who provided both emotional support and intellectual stimulation. These relationships were not transactional; they were built on mutual respect, love, and shared values. Maya Angelou often reflected on how her circle of relationships shaped her resilience and ability to inspire others.

Angelou's relationships highlight how essential it is to surround yourself with people who lift you up, push you to grow, and offer emotional and intellectual nourishment. It is through nurturing these meaningful connections that we can endure life's hardships and rise to our greatest potential.

Maya Angelou's relationships were built on mutual growth and respect. These connections didn't just support her—they helped her, and those around her, grow into better versions of themselves.

Ask Yourself: *If Maya Angelou could rise above hardships through the power of supportive connections, what relationships in your life can you nurture to help you grow?*

Key Components of Meaningful Relationships

1. **Communication**: Effective communication is the lifeblood of any relationship. Active listening, empathy, and honesty are cornerstones of healthy communication. Superheroes often share open lines of communication with their allies to work as a cohesive team—this is no different in personal relationships.
2. **Trust**: Trust is built through consistent, reliable behavior over time. Relationships built on trust provide security and emotional stability, essential for long-term personal growth.
3. **Empathy**: Empathy allows us to connect on a deeper level with others by understanding their feelings and perspectives. It builds emotional bonds and fosters mutual respect, making relationships more resilient.
4. **Support**: Meaningful relationships are those where support flows both ways. Whether in good times or bad, true connections involve offering help when needed and accepting help with gratitude when offered.
5. **Respect**: Respecting boundaries, differences in opinion, and individuality are key to maintaining relationships where both parties feel valued and heard.

"Alone we can do so little; together we can do so much."

– Helen Keller

The Value of Time Over Money

In our busy lives, it's easy to get caught up in the hustle, telling ourselves that we're working hard for the people we love. We may say, "I'll spend time with my family when I have more free time," or, "I'm doing all of this for them."

But the reality is, money cannot replace the time, love, and attention that our relationships need to thrive.

Imagine you've worked late into the night all week, thinking you're doing it for your family's financial stability. But when was the last time you had a meaningful conversation with your partner or shared a simple, joyful moment with your children? While work is essential, so is carving out time to be fully present with the people who matter most.

Quality time fosters strong emotional bonds, brings joy, and enhances the longevity of meaningful relationships. As the *Harvard Study* shows, it's not money or success that brings lasting happiness—it's connection.

Call to Reflection and Action

Nurturing relationships is about taking proactive steps to strengthen your emotional bonds. Whether it's a family member, friend, or colleague, take a moment to reflect on how you're investing in your relationships and what small changes you can make to improve them.

Ask Yourself:

1. Who in your life brings you the most joy and support?
2. Are there any relationships in your life that could benefit from more attention or effort?
3. What can you do today to strengthen one of your most meaningful connections?

Time to Take Action

1. **Gratitude Exercise**: Choose one person in your life who has significantly impacted you. Write them a heartfelt letter expressing gratitude for their presence and support. Even if you don't send it, this exercise will help you reflect on the importance of the people in your life.

   Example: You might write to your best friend: 'I'm so grateful for your unwavering support during my difficult times. You've helped me find strength when I felt like giving up, and I cherish every moment we've shared.' Even if you don't send it, this exercise helps you appreciate the role they play in your life."

2. **Reconnect Exercise**: Make it a point to reconnect with someone important to you whom you haven't spoken to in a while. Set a date for a coffee chat, a video call, or a simple phone conversation to catch up and renew your bond.

Final Thoughts

Building and maintaining meaningful relationships is a powerful, ongoing process. Strong connections are vital to our emotional and mental well-being, helping us navigate life's joys and challenges. Just as superheroes lean on their team of allies, you too must nurture your own team—family, friends, and community. By investing time, attention, and care into your relationships, you can create a support system that sustains you through life's adventures.

The key to unlocking your inner superhero lies not just within you but also in the relationships you cultivate. Embrace these connections, invest in them, and watch as your personal growth and happiness expand in extraordinary ways.

Chapter 08

THE IMPORTANCE OF COMMUNITY

"I alone cannot change the world, but I can cast a stone across the waters to create many ripples."

– Mother Teresa

The Role of Community in Holistic Living

Community is one of the cornerstones of personal well-being and holistic living. Just as superheroes rely on their teams—whether it's the Avengers, the Justice League, or the X-Men—to support them through challenges, we too benefit from the strength of our community. Beyond individual heroism, strong relationships and collective action lead to lasting success.

Being part of a supportive, diverse, and engaged community allows us to draw emotional strength, wisdom, and collective power that helps us thrive. Communities offer shared growth, accountability, and support. They foster personal fulfillment, improve mental health, and provide the connection we need to face life's challenges.

"Community is where individual strengths merge to create something greater than the sum of its parts."

– Author

Be Your Own Superhero: Building and Engaging with Community

To fully unlock your inner superhero, it's crucial to recognise that you are not alone on this journey. The people you surround yourself with—family, friends, colleagues, neighbours—form the community that uplifts, inspires, and supports you. Meaningful engagement with your community not only enhances your personal life but also provides opportunities to give back, make a difference, and strengthen society.

Like superheroes who assemble a team to face adversity, you can take active steps to build and engage with a community that reflects your values and offers the collective strength needed to flourish.

Sometimes, becoming an active part of your community means stepping out of your comfort zone. Whether it's joining a new group or offering help, these small acts can lead to deeper connections and a stronger support system.

The Science Behind Community and Well-being

Scientific studies underscore the importance of community in promoting mental and physical health. Research from *PLOS Medicine* shows that people with strong social connections have a 50% higher likelihood of living longer compared to those with weaker ties. Another study from *Harvard University* reveals that belonging to a community reduces stress, enhances immune function, and promotes overall well-being.

In today's fast-paced world, where loneliness and social isolation are becoming more prevalent, building strong and meaningful connections is more vital than ever. Engaging in your community provides a sense of purpose, reduces loneliness, and increases resilience in the face of life's challenges.

While local communities provide essential in-person support, online communities can also offer a sense of belonging and connection, especially for those who might not have easy access to physical groups. Virtual networks can help combat isolation and offer diverse perspectives from around the world.

Case Study: The Collective Power of Ubuntu in South Africa

An inspiring example of community strength is the African concept of **Ubuntu**—a philosophy that emphasises interconnectedness and the belief that "I am because we are." Ubuntu became globally recognised during South Africa's post-apartheid transition, where community healing and reconciliation were paramount. Archbishop **Desmond Tutu** popularized this concept, advocating that every person's humanity is tied to the humanity of others.

Ubuntu teaches that community is essential to well-being. No one can truly thrive in isolation. By acknowledging the impact of our actions on others, the South African community came together to rebuild a nation fractured by decades of violence and hatred. The philosophy of Ubuntu shows how communities, when driven by shared values and mutual respect, can foster peace, growth, and collective resilience.

Ask Yourself: *If South Africans could come together to rebuild after decades of division and conflict, how can you contribute to building a stronger, more supportive community around you?*

Key Components of Building a Strong Community

1. **Connection**: Meaningful relationships are built through active listening, empathy, and genuine interest in others. True connection forms the foundation of any strong community.
2. **Collaboration**: Communities thrive when individuals work together toward shared goals. Collaboration fosters creativity, problem-solving, and growth.
3. **Contribution**: Offering your time, skills, or resources to your community helps build bonds and creates a shared sense of purpose. Acts of kindness, volunteering, and simply being present for others strengthen the social fabric of any group.
4. **Support**: Emotional and practical support within a community fosters resilience. Offering help to others—and receiving it when you need it—creates bonds of trust and deepens relationships.

5. **Diversity and Inclusion**: Embracing diversity strengthens communities by bringing together varied perspectives, experiences, and strengths. Inclusion ensures that everyone has a voice and feels valued.

"Never doubt that a small group of thoughtful, committed citizens can change the world; indeed, it's the only thing that ever has."

– Margaret Mead

The Value of Giving and Receiving Support

Communities flourish when there's an open exchange of support. However, many people hesitate to ask for help, feeling that doing so shows weakness or imposes a burden. The truth is, seeking help strengthens the bonds within a community. In the same way superheroes call upon their teams for assistance, you should feel empowered to reach out when needed.

Imagine how different your life would be if you fully embraced both giving and receiving support within your community. By engaging in these mutual exchanges, you not only build stronger relationships but also contribute to a culture of care and collaboration.

Contributing to your community doesn't just strengthen relationships—it also provides a sense of fulfillment and purpose. By giving your time and support, you'll find that the emotional rewards are just as valuable as what you offer.

Ask Yourself:

1. What communities are you currently part of, and how do they support your well-being?
2. How can you contribute more effectively to your community, both locally and globally?
3. What steps can you take to build new, meaningful connections within your community?

Time to Take Action

1. **Community Assessment**: Reflect on your current communities—whether they are social, professional, or local groups. Identify areas where you can engage more or where you might seek new communities that align with your values and interests.

2. **Contribution Plan**: Think about how you can actively contribute to your community. Write down ways you can offer your time, skills, or resources. For example, volunteering, organizing an event, or mentoring a young person. Set a goal to act on one of these ideas in the next month.

Final Thoughts

Building and engaging with a strong community is essential for living a fulfilling and resilient life. Communities provide not only companionship but also a sense of shared purpose, opportunities for growth, and emotional strength. They give us a platform to make a difference, amplify our impact, and sustain us through life's challenges.

By nurturing relationships, contributing to collective goals, and embracing diversity, you will experience both personal and shared transformation. Together with your community, you can make a powerful and lasting impact on the world.

Section 4

Goal Setting and Personal Growth

Chapter 09

SETTING CLEAR GOALS AND FINDING YOUR PATH

"What you get by achieving your goals is not as important as what you become by achieving your goals."

– Zig Ziglar

The Power of Goal Setting

Setting clear goals is foundational to success and living a life of purpose. Think of superheroes—they always have a clear mission, whether it's saving the world or protecting their community. This mission drives their every action. In the same way, setting defined, purposeful goals provides direction, motivation, and a sense of achievement as you progress through life. Without goals, you're like a ship adrift without a course.

Be Your Own Superhero: Defining Your Mission

To tap into your inner superhero, you must define your mission. This is done through setting clear, meaningful goals that align with your core values and long-term aspirations. Just as superheroes focus on their mission with unwavering determination, you too can bring focus and energy to your life through goal setting. Your goals are your map; they guide you through uncertainties, keeping you aligned with your purpose.

Sometimes, life's challenges or self-doubt can cloud your vision, making it hard to see your mission clearly. Revisiting and refining your goals allows you to adapt, realign with your values, and continue moving forward with purpose.

"Goals are the compass that guide your actions and transform dreams into reality. Without them, you're just drifting—find your path and follow it with purpose."

– Author

The Science Behind Goal Setting

Goal setting is not just about making a to-do list—research shows it's one of the most effective ways to drive success. According to Dr. Gail Matthews from Dominican University of California, individuals who write down their goals, share them, and provide regular updates are 33% more likely to achieve them than those who don't. This highlights the importance of clarity, commitment, and accountability in the goal-setting process.

The Need for Goal Setting

Imagine calling a cab, sitting inside, and when the driver asks where you're headed, you simply say, "Anywhere." The driver, understandably confused, won't know where to take you, and you'll likely end up nowhere. Isn't this the same when we live life without clear goals? Drifting aimlessly, unsure of our purpose or where we're headed.

Setting goals provides direction. It helps you determine not only *what* you want but *how* you'll achieve it. Imagine waking up each day with a clear sense of purpose, knowing exactly what steps you need to take. Your goals become the compass guiding you through life, offering clarity and focus, even in times of uncertainty.

Goals aren't just destinations—they're also the journey. Think of them as landmarks along the path of your life, each representing growth, learning, and progress. With every goal you achieve, you become stronger, more resilient, and closer to living the life you truly desire.

Without clear goals, we may feel stuck, frustrated, or overwhelmed by uncertainty. Setting purposeful goals alleviates these feelings by giving you a sense of control and momentum in life.

"Clear goals are the stepping stones to greatness. Each one brings you closer to the version of yourself you're meant to become."

– Author

Case Study: Elon Musk's Mission-Oriented Goals

Elon Musk, the visionary entrepreneur behind SpaceX, Tesla, and SolarCity, provides a compelling example of mission-driven goal setting. Musk's overarching mission—ushering in a sustainable future for humanity—guides all his actions. His goals aren't just about making electric cars or launching rockets; they align with his larger vision of reducing humanity's carbon footprint and enabling life on other planets.

Musk's success wasn't achieved overnight. It's the result of breaking down monumental goals into smaller, measurable steps. Whether launching the first reusable rocket or mass-producing electric cars, Musk sets time-bound, challenging yet achievable goals. His relentless focus on the larger mission, combined with smaller, actionable steps, has made him one of the most influential visionaries of our time.

This serves as a reminder: your goals should be grounded in your mission and broken down into actionable steps. When your goals are tied to a larger purpose, they give your life direction, fuel your motivation, and sustain you through challenges.

Musk's ability to adapt his goals and pivot when necessary—whether it was shifting timelines or refining his vision—has been a crucial part of his success.

Flexibility, combined with relentless focus, has allowed him to overcome obstacles and stay aligned with his mission.

Ask Yourself: *If Elon could achieve such monumental goals through focus and persistence, what mission or purpose drives you?*

Key Components of Effective Goal Setting

1. **Clarity**: Clearly defined goals provide a specific direction and enable you to create a plan of action. Vague goals lack the focus needed to guide your efforts.
2. **Measurability**: Setting measurable goals helps you track progress and stay motivated. Define specific criteria for success so you can evaluate your achievements.
3. **Achievability**: Goals should be challenging yet attainable. Setting unrealistic goals may lead to frustration, while realistic goals inspire confidence and drive.
4. **Relevance**: Your goals should align with your values, passions, and long-term aspirations. Relevant goals ensure your efforts are meaningful and rewarding.
5. **Time-Bound**: Goals should have deadlines. Without a time frame, goals may lose their urgency and become susceptible to procrastination.

While goals should be time-bound and measurable, it's also important to remain flexible. Life circumstances may shift, and adapting your goals allows you to stay committed to your mission without feeling discouraged.

"Setting goals is the first step in turning the invisible into the visible."

– Tony Robbins

Ask Yourself:

1. What are your current goals, and how well do they align with your core values and aspirations?
2. Are your goals specific, measurable, and time-bound? How can you make them more actionable?
3. How will achieving these goals contribute to your overall well-being and personal growth?

Time to Take Action

1. **Goal Reflection**: Take time to reflect on what truly matters to you. Write down one short-term and one long-term goals that are SMART (Specific, Measurable, Achievable, Relevant, and Time-bound). Review and refine your goals until they align with your core values and aspirations.

2. **Action Plan Creation**: Break down each goal into smaller steps. What can you do today, this week, or this month to move closer to your goal? Document your plan, adding deadlines to each step, and review it regularly.

   Example: If your goal is to run a marathon, start by setting smaller milestones: run 1 mile a day this week, increase to 2 miles next week, and gradually build up to longer distances. Setting deadlines for each step will keep you on track and motivated.

Final Thoughts

Setting clear goals is like becoming the superhero of your own life. It's not just about what you achieve, but who you become through the process. Every step you take toward your goal strengthens your resilience, determination, and focus.

By defining your mission, creating a roadmap, and staying committed to your action plan, you'll transform aimless aspirations into purposeful achievements. Like Elon Musk's vision of the future, your goals should be part of a larger mission—one that inspires and challenges you every day.

The path to personal greatness starts with a single step. Don't leave your life to chance. Chart your course, take control, and move with purpose. Embrace the journey, knowing that each goal you set and achieve brings you closer to unlocking your inner superhero.

Chapter 10

LIVING WITH PURPOSE

"Those who have a 'why' to live, can bear with almost any 'how.'"

– Viktor Frankl

The Importance of Purpose

Living with purpose is a key element of a fulfilling and balanced life. Much like superheroes, who are driven by clear missions and a higher calling, having a sense of purpose gives meaning to our actions and clarity to our decisions. Purpose is what fuels resilience during challenging times and brings fulfillment to moments of success. When your life is guided by purpose, every action feels intentional, aligned with your deepest values and passions.

But purpose is not just a lofty ideal; it's a practical foundation for daily living. It is the driving force that can turn mundane tasks into meaningful experiences and hardships into stepping stones for growth. Discovering and embracing your purpose transforms your life from reactive to intentional, from drifting to directed.

"Purpose gives your actions meaning, your challenges strength, and your life direction. Without it, you're simply moving, but with it, you're truly living."

– Author

Be Your Own Superhero: Discovering and Living Your Purpose

To be your own superhero, discovering and living your purpose is essential. Like superheroes with clear missions, you too need a personal mission that aligns with your values, passions, and strengths. Living with purpose doesn't just happen—it's a conscious choice that requires reflection, action, and continuous alignment with what truly matters to you. When you live with purpose, even the smallest actions contribute to a greater sense of fulfillment.

Imagine waking up each morning with a clear understanding of why you're doing what you're doing. Your purpose serves as a compass, guiding your decisions and keeping you focused on what's truly important.

Remember, purpose is not static. As you grow and experience life, your purpose may evolve. Stay open to change, and allow your mission to adapt as you gain new insights and experiences

The Science Behind Living with Purpose

A striking example of the power of purpose comes from the village of Ogimi in Okinawa, Japan. Known for having one of the highest concentrations of centenarians in the world, the residents of Ogimi attribute their longevity not only to healthy living but also to a profound sense of purpose. In Ogimi, the concept of retirement doesn't exist in the traditional sense. Instead, residents live with a strong *ikigai*—a Japanese term that means "reason for being." This *ikigai* keeps them engaged, active, and deeply connected to their community.

One key factor behind their extended lifespans is the fact that even into their later years, they contribute meaningfully to their society through activities such as farming, caregiving, or community leadership. Each day, they wake up with something to strive for, a task that gives them meaning and connects them with the world around them. Their sense of purpose is intertwined with a strong community bond, which supports their emotional and mental well-being.

The lesson here is profound: living with purpose does more than just give us direction—it sustains life itself. Purpose acts as the fuel that energizes us to keep going, no matter our age or circumstances. It allows us to turn our daily routines into opportunities for growth and connection.

Now, consider your own *ikigai*. What gives you a reason to get up in the morning? What fills your life with meaning? By identifying and nurturing this sense of purpose, you too can live a life full of vitality and fulfillment.

Purpose isn't found only in big, life-altering missions. It's also in the small, daily actions—whether it's helping a neighbour, improving your health, or learning something new. These moments, when aligned with your values, are what build a life of purpose.

"When you align your actions with your purpose, even the smallest tasks can lead you towards a life of fulfillment."

– Author

Key Components of Living with Purpose

1. **Self-Discovery**: Discovering your purpose starts with understanding who you are. Reflect on your core values, passions, and strengths. What activities energize you? What gives you a sense of meaning and fulfillment?
2. **Goal Setting**: Once you've identified your purpose, set meaningful and specific goals that align with it. These goals provide direction and motivation, helping you focus your efforts on what truly matters.
3. **Aligning Actions with Values**: Living with purpose means ensuring that your daily actions reflect your values. Ask yourself if your habits and routines contribute to your long-term goals and fulfillment.
4. **Contributing to a Greater Good**: Purpose often extends beyond personal goals. It involves contributing to something bigger than yourself, whether through your work, community involvement, or acts of kindness. Finding ways to give back amplifies your sense of purpose.

5. **Continuous Reflection and Adjustment**: Purpose evolves over time, and so should your goals. Regular reflection helps you stay aligned with your evolving values and aspirations, allowing you to adjust your path when needed.

"The purpose of life is not to be happy. It is to be useful, to be honourable, to be compassionate, to have it make some difference that you have lived and lived well."

– Ralph Waldo Emerson

Practical Case Study: The Story of Jane Goodall

Jane Goodall's life provides a powerful example of living with purpose. Known for her groundbreaking work with chimpanzees in Tanzania, Goodall has dedicated her entire life to wildlife conservation and environmental activism. Her sense of purpose is deeply connected to her love for animals and her commitment to understanding and protecting the natural world.

Despite facing numerous challenges—being a young woman in a male-dominated field, working in remote locations, and dealing with funding difficulties—Goodall's unwavering sense of purpose drove her to continue her research and advocacy. She has since founded the Jane Goodall Institute, which works to protect wildlife and promote environmental conservation globally.

Goodall's story shows that when we live with purpose, we find resilience in the face of adversity. Our purpose becomes a source of strength that keeps us going, even when the road ahead seems difficult. What drives you, like Jane Goodall, to make a lasting impact on the world?

Ask Yourself: *If Jane Goodall could overcome her challenges to make a global impact on wildlife conservation, what's stopping you from pursuing your own passion and making a difference?*

Ask Yourself

1. What are your core values and passions?
2. How do your current actions align with your values and purpose?
3. What changes can you make to live more purposefully?

Time to Take Action

1. **SMART Goal Setting**: Identify one or two key goals that align with your purpose and make them SMART (Specific, Measurable, Achievable, Relevant, and Time-bound). Outline the steps you'll take to achieve them.

   Example: If your purpose is to contribute to environmental conservation, a SMART goal might be: 'I will volunteer with a local environmental group for 5 hours a month for the next six months, and work on educating others about sustainability practices.'

2. **Contribution to a Greater Good**: Research volunteer opportunities, join a cause you believe in, or simply practice acts of kindness. Find ways to contribute to something larger than yourself, whether through your work, community service, or personal actions.

Final Thoughts

Living with purpose is the cornerstone of a meaningful life. Just as superheroes are driven by a sense of duty and mission, you too can discover and live your purpose by aligning your actions with your values, setting meaningful goals, and contributing to the greater good. This not only enhances your personal fulfillment but also allows you to make a positive impact on the world around you.

By consistently reflecting on your purpose, adjusting your path when necessary, and staying true to your values, you can live a life filled with passion and significance. Your purpose is the key to unlocking your full potential and leading a truly rewarding life.

Chapter 11

MASTERING THE ART OF DECISION MAKING

"It is in your moments of decision that your destiny is shaped."

– Tony Robbins

The Power of Decisions

The decisions we make shape our lives. Superheroes often stand at crossroads, faced with critical decisions that determine the outcome of their missions and the lives of others. Similarly, in our everyday lives, each decision we make—no matter how small—has the potential to shape our future, affect our well-being, and contribute to our success.

Mastering the art of decision-making is more than just learning how to make choices; it's about developing the confidence to act decisively and understanding the broader impact of each decision on your life's journey. When we master decision-making, we empower ourselves to live with purpose and intention, taking control of the path we are forging.

Be Your Own Superhero: Making Empowered Decisions

To be your own superhero, you must master decision-making by aligning your choices with your values and long-term goals. Superheroes, despite their powers, understand that their decisions carry weight and responsibility. In the same way, you can become a decision-making superhero by cultivating clarity, gathering relevant information, weighing options, and trusting your intuition. When decisions are made with purpose and confidence, they propel you forward on your journey to self-mastery and fulfillment.

Effective decision-making requires understanding the impact of each choice, learning from past experiences, and using that knowledge to make empowered decisions. By doing so, you can navigate life's challenges with clarity and confidence, ensuring that your decisions move you closer to your goals.

Fear is often the silent companion to big decisions, but true empowerment comes when you learn to move forward despite it. Every bold choice builds courage, making each subsequent decision easier to navigate with confidence.

"Mastering decisions means trusting your intuition, learning from the past, and embracing the unknown with confidence."

– Author

The Science Behind Decision Making

Research demonstrates that structured decision-making enhances both satisfaction and success. For instance, a study in the *Journal of Behavioral Decision Making* showed that people who employ structured decision-making strategies experience reduced stress and higher satisfaction. Another study by the American Psychological Association stressed the importance of combining rational thinking with intuition for sound decision-making.

Interestingly, neuroscientists have discovered that while our brain's logical, rational centres guide many decisions, our emotions play an equally important role in the process. This balance of logic and intuition can help us arrive at decisions that not only make sense but feel right. So, trusting your intuition when it aligns with your values can be just as crucial as gathering facts.

In today's fast-paced world, decision fatigue can deplete your mental energy, making it harder to make sound choices. By simplifying routine decisions—like what to wear or eat—you can preserve mental clarity for the decisions that truly matter.

The Impact of Decision Making in Our Lives

Consider the adage: *"We are what we decide."* Reflect on your current life—your health, wealth, relationships, and professional achievements. Every aspect of your current reality is shaped by a series of decisions you've made, whether consciously or subconsciously. Like connecting the dots, each choice has led you to where you are today.

If you struggle with certain aspects of your life—be it financial trouble, health challenges, or relationship struggles—it's worth retracing your decisions. Was there a time when you chose short-term convenience over long-term benefit? For instance, indulging in unhealthy food choices over time may have led to physical challenges. Or perhaps a hasty decision in a relationship or investment caused avoidable turmoil.

Our lives are essentially the sum of our decisions, big and small. That one choice to take a leap of faith—or, conversely, the decision to stay in our comfort zone—carries significant weight over time. The power of decision-making, then, is not just in the major life choices, but in the smaller, everyday decisions that accumulate over time to shape our destiny.

Not Taking A Decision Is Also A Decision

When we face difficult decisions, it's common to delay or avoid making them out of fear or uncertainty. However, not making a decision is a decision in itself. Indecision leads to stagnation, preventing progress and change.

Imagine standing at a crossroads, unsure of which path to take. While one path may lead to an unexpected challenge and the other to success, choosing to stand still guarantees that you go nowhere. You miss out on both the lessons and opportunities that action brings. The fear of making the wrong decision often keeps us stuck, but the risk of inaction is far greater: it ensures that nothing changes.

The next time you hesitate, remember that indecision is a decision—one that robs you of growth. Even if the decision you make turns out to be less than perfect, it is still an opportunity to learn, adapt, and move forward.

Overthinking is one of the biggest barriers to decision-making. To combat it, set a time limit for making your choice. Giving yourself a deadline forces action and reduces the risk of getting stuck in indecision.

"Indecision is the enemy of progress. Trust yourself, make the call, and let every choice be a bold move toward the life you want."

– Author

Key Components of Decision Making

1. **Clarity of Values and Goals**: Knowing your core values and long-term objectives serves as a compass for making informed decisions. When your decisions align with your values, you are more likely to make choices that bring satisfaction and fulfillment.
2. **Gathering Information**: Effective decisions are rooted in knowledge. Collect relevant information and consider multiple perspectives before making a choice. This includes research, seeking advice, and weighing the options available.
3. **Weighing Pros and Cons**: Taking time to analyze the potential benefits and risks of each option gives clarity. By making a pros and cons list, you can evaluate the impact of your decision in an organised way.
4. **Trusting Intuition**: While rational analysis is essential, intuition also plays a significant role. Trust your gut feelings, especially when they align with your past experiences and core values. Intuition can often lead you toward the most authentic decision.

5. **Learning from Experience**: Each decision offers an opportunity to reflect and grow. Whether your choices lead to success or failure, taking time to assess the outcome can sharpen your future decision-making skills.

Case Study: Steve Jobs and the Power of Intuition

Steve Jobs, the co-founder of Apple, is often celebrated for his groundbreaking innovations and business acumen. However, one of the lesser-known aspects of his decision-making process was his reliance on intuition. Jobs famously said, *"Have the courage to follow your heart and intuition. They somehow already know what you truly want to become."*

One key example of Jobs' intuitive decision-making was his choice to leave college early. Despite societal pressure to complete formal education, Jobs felt that traditional schooling wasn't aligned with his personal goals. Following his intuition, he dropped out and later audited classes that interested him—such as calligraphy, which eventually influenced the typography of Apple's first computers.

Jobs' decision to trust his gut wasn't just a one-time occurrence; it became a hallmark of his leadership style. From the development of the iPhone to his insistence on user-friendly design, Jobs made many business decisions based not solely on market research or logic, but on intuition and a deep understanding of what felt right for the company and its vision.

His story is a testament to the importance of listening to your inner voice, especially when it aligns with your goals and values.

Jobs' decision-making process wasn't just about following intuition blindly—it was about integrating his gut feelings with a calculated assessment of risks and possibilities. This balance allowed him to make bold yet informed decisions that shaped his legacy.

Ask Yourself: *If Steve Jobs could trust his intuition to make bold decisions that revolutionized entire industries, what's stopping you from following your own inner voice to pursue your goals and passions?*

Ask Yourself

1. What core values guide your decisions?
2. How do you balance rational analysis and intuition in your decision-making process?
3. Reflect on a recent decision you made. What did you learn from the outcome?

Time to Take Action

1. **Pros and Cons List**: For an upcoming decision, create a detailed list of pros and cons for each option. Use this list to evaluate which choice aligns best with your goals.

   Example: If you're deciding whether to switch careers, list pros such as 'new opportunities, more fulfilling work, higher salary,' and cons such as 'initial uncertainty, leaving a stable job, adjusting to a new environment.' Seeing the benefits and risks laid out can bring clarity to your decision."

2. **Take Decisive Action**: When faced with an upcoming decision, evaluate your options, trust your intuition, and then take action with confidence. Learn to embrace both the potential for success and the lessons of failure.

Final Thoughts

Mastering the art of decision-making is a pivotal step in becoming your own superhero. By clarifying your values, gathering information, analyzing your options, and trusting your intuition, you can make empowered choices that shape your future. The key is to act with intention, learn from each decision, and continuously refine your process. Embrace each decision as a powerful opportunity to shape your destiny, and let your life be guided by the clarity and confidence that come from mastering this essential skill.

Section 5

Balance Work and Time Management

Chapter 12

ACHIEVING BALANCE BETWEEN WORK AND LIFE

"The key is not to prioritise what's on your schedule, but to schedule your priorities."

– Stephen Covey

The Importance of Work-Life Balance

Work-life balance is vital for maintaining overall well-being and happiness. Superheroes, while saving the world, often face the challenge of balancing their public missions with their private lives. In a similar vein, achieving a balance between your professional and personal responsibilities is essential for reducing stress, fostering meaningful relationships, and ensuring long-term success.

Without balance, we risk burnout, deteriorating health, and strained relationships. Striving for harmony between work and life allows you to not only thrive professionally but also nurture your personal life, passions, and well-being. It's about finding that sweet spot where both aspects coexist, enriching each other rather than competing.

Be Your Own Superhero: Striving for Work-Life Balance

To be your own superhero, mastering the art of balance is crucial. This requires setting clear boundaries, prioritising self-care, and learning to manage your time effectively. Just like superheroes maintain their strength by managing their dual lives, you too can thrive by creating a sustainable balance between work and personal life.

Achieving this balance empowers you to lead a fulfilled life where both your career and personal relationships can grow in harmony, giving you energy and purpose rather than leaving you feeling overextended and overwhelmed.

Balance isn't static. There will be times when work demands more of you, and other times when your personal life takes priority. The key is to remain adaptable, knowing that balance is about adjusting and realigning as needed.

The Science Behind Work-Life Balance

Research underscores the importance of work-life balance for both physical and mental health. A study published in the *Journal of Occupational Health Psychology* revealed that individuals who maintain a healthy balance between work and personal life experience lower stress levels, better job satisfaction, and enhanced overall health. Additionally, research by the American Psychological Association found that work-life balance is directly linked to increased productivity, higher morale, and reduced burnout.

The benefits extend beyond individual well-being—organisations that support employees in achieving work-life balance see higher engagement, creativity, and retention rates. Ultimately, balance isn't just good for personal health; it's crucial for success in every area of life.

In today's digitally connected world, setting digital boundaries—such as turning off work emails and social media after hours—can significantly improve work-life balance. By disconnecting from work during personal time, you can recharge more effectively and return to work with renewed focus.

Personal Story: Breaking Free from the Work-Life Tug-of-War

Years ago, I found myself in a relentless cycle, trying to juggle the demands of my business with my family life. I was deeply engrossed in running my logistics company, with non-stop calls, emails, and unexpected crises dominating my days. Even weekends and holidays were taken over by work. While physically present with my family, my mind was always tethered to my phone or laptop.

It wasn't long before this imbalance took a toll. I was missing out on important family moments, feeling disconnected, and my health was suffering due to constant stress. My family was supportive but quietly frustrated by my constant absence, and I was overwhelmed by the demands of my business, always on the edge of burnout.

One day, it hit me hard: If I didn't make a change, I risked losing everything that truly mattered. That realisation marked a turning point. I started setting clear boundaries between work and personal time. I set aside specific, non-negotiable times for family and rest. Although breaking my old habits was difficult at first, the change was transformative.

As I committed to these boundaries, my stress levels decreased, and I became more present for my family. My relationships improved, and my health rebounded. I also noticed that I was more productive and focused at work, no longer feeling like I was constantly putting out fires. This journey taught me that balance isn't a luxury—it's a necessity for long-term happiness and success.

If you're feeling like I once did—overworked and stretched thin—know that achieving balance is possible. It requires setting priorities, clear boundaries, and committing to them. Balance isn't about perfection; it's about making intentional choices to lead a fulfilling life both at work and home.

"Balance isn't about dividing your time equally—it's about aligning your actions with your priorities so both your work and life can thrive."

– Author

Key Components of Achieving Work-Life Balance

1. **Time Management**: Effective time management helps you prioritise tasks, set realistic goals, and allocate your time wisely between work, family, and personal activities. By creating structured plans, you can avoid feeling overwhelmed and make space for what truly matters.
2. **Setting Boundaries**: Healthy boundaries ensure that work doesn't consume your entire life. Setting clear limits on when and where you work allows you to recharge and focus on your personal life, ultimately benefiting both your professional and personal well-being.
3. **Self-Care**: Taking care of yourself—mentally, physically, and emotionally—is essential for maintaining balance. Prioritise activities like exercise, hobbies, rest, and personal growth to keep yourself rejuvenated and focused.
4. **Flexibility and Adaptability**: Life is unpredictable, and achieving balance requires flexibility. Being open to adjusting your plans, expectations, and routines in response to changing circumstances helps you maintain balance through life's inevitable disruptions.

Case Study: Sheryl Sandberg's Path to Balance

Sheryl Sandberg, the COO of Facebook and author of *Lean In*, is a prime example of someone who has publicly shared her struggles with work-life balance. In her early years at Facebook, Sandberg was known for leaving the office at 5:30 p.m. to spend time with her family. Despite the high-pressure demands of her job, she made it clear that her family came first, even if it meant doing work from home after her children went to bed.

This choice to prioritise family didn't hinder her career; instead, it made her a role model for professionals seeking balance. Sandberg openly advocates for setting boundaries and encourages other working professionals to do the same. Her transparency about managing both work and life has helped pave the way for others to follow suit.

Sandberg's story demonstrates that achieving work-life balance doesn't mean sacrificing your career. Rather, it's about creating a system that works for your personal and professional goals.

Sandberg's decision to leave work at 5:30 p.m. was not only a personal boundary but a challenge to the prevailing work culture, encouraging others to confidently prioritize their personal lives without sacrificing career success.

Ask Yourself: *If Sheryl Sandberg could set boundaries and prioritize her family while excelling in her career, what's stopping you from creating your own work-life balance?*

Ask Yourself

1. What are your top priorities in life, and how do they align with your current schedule?
2. How can you create a balanced schedule that includes time for work, family, self-care, and leisure?
3. What self-care activities can you incorporate into your daily routine to reduce stress and increase well-being?

Time to Take Action

1. **Balanced Schedule Creation**: Develop a balanced schedule for your daily or weekly routine. Ensure it includes time for work, personal commitments, family, self-care, and leisure. Stick to this schedule, and allow it to evolve as needed.

   Example: For example, you might block out time from 6-8 p.m. for family activities, 7-8 a.m. for exercise, and leave work hours strictly between 9 a.m. and 5 p.m., with a 15-minute break every two hours to recharge. Setting these boundaries will help you allocate time more effectively.

2. **Self-Care Plan**: Create a personalised self-care plan that includes activities you enjoy, such as exercise, meditation, reading, or hobbies. Schedule these activities regularly and treat them as essential, non-negotiable parts of your routine.

Final Thoughts

Achieving balance between work and life is a vital step in becoming your own superhero. By managing your time effectively, setting clear boundaries, and prioritising self-care, you can reduce stress, improve your relationships, and boost your productivity. Remember, balance isn't a one-time achievement—it's a continual process of adjusting and aligning your actions with your priorities. Embrace this journey toward balance, and watch as it transforms not only your professional success but also your personal fulfillment.

Chapter 13

MASTERING TIME MANAGEMENT FOR A PRODUCTIVE LIFE

"Lost time is never found again."

– Benjamin Franklin

The Value of Time Management

Time management is a critical skill that helps you make the most of your time, achieve your goals, and maintain balance in life. Much like superheroes, who must juggle their responsibilities of saving the world and living their personal lives, mastering time management enables you to excel in both your professional and personal domains. By organising your time effectively, you can increase productivity, reduce stress, and lead a more fulfilling life.

"Time is your most valuable asset—guard it with purpose, spend it with intention, and invest it in what truly matters."

– Author

Be Your Own Superhero: Mastering Time Management

To be your own superhero, you need to master time management. This isn't just about squeezing more into your day; it's about making better use of the time you have. Superheroes achieve their missions by prioritising their actions, managing resources, and staying focused. In the same way, you must structure your day, prioritise important tasks, and stay disciplined in order to achieve your goals and live a balanced life.

The Science Behind Time Management

Research shows that mastering time management is directly linked to increased productivity, improved mental health, and greater life satisfaction. A study published in the *Journal of Applied Psychology* found that people who actively practice time management experience lower stress levels and higher job satisfaction. The *American Psychological Association* also found that effective time management contributes to better work-life balance, reducing the likelihood of burnout and increasing overall well-being.

Research also shows that multitasking, while seemingly productive, often results in less efficient use of time. By focusing on one task at a time, you increase your ability to complete work faster and with higher quality.

Time as a Concept

You might be thinking: *Not another chapter on time management.* But let's shift the lens—this isn't just a standard "plan your day" conversation. In fact, I want to suggest something radical: *You can't manage time*. Time, by definition, is the continuous, unstoppable flow of events from the past through the present into the future. We can't control time itself.

What we can manage is *ourselves* within the time we have. Time is a precious, finite resource, and it's slipping away every moment. The question isn't how to stop or manage time; it's how to use it wisely, with intent and purpose. This chapter will help you rethink how you spend your time, giving you tools to make conscious decisions that reflect your priorities.

Why Time Matters So Much

We often treat time as if we have an endless supply. We procrastinate, let distractions eat away at our days, and delay important tasks with the assumption that more time will come tomorrow. The reality is that time is finite. Every second you spend is gone forever—how you spend it shapes your future.

Mastering time management means taking control of *your actions* within the time you have. It's about making thoughtful choices that reflect your priorities so that you can look back without regret. When you manage your time effectively, you're managing your life. Time invested in purposeful activities builds a life of meaning, whether you're working toward career goals, nurturing relationships, or simply enjoying the present moment.

Key Components of Time Management

1. **Prioritisation**: Identify and focus on your most important tasks. Prioritising helps you allocate your time and energy to activities that align with your long-term goals and values.
2. **Planning**: A structured schedule allows you to stay organised and make time for all aspects of life—work, rest, personal growth, and recreation.
3. **Goal Setting**: Clear, achievable goals provide motivation and a sense of direction. By setting measurable goals, you stay focused and can track your progress.
4. **Delegation**: Handing off tasks when appropriate allows you to manage your workload better, enabling you to focus on high-priority tasks. Delegation increases overall productivity.
5. **Time Blocking**: Setting specific time blocks for tasks helps you stay focused and avoid distractions. This approach ensures that each task gets adequate attention without overwhelming you.

The Value of Your Time

Let's get practical. Imagine you earn ₹42 lakhs annually. Breaking that down into an hourly rate, assuming you work eight hours a day, five days a week, your productive time is worth roughly ₹2,000 per hour. Now, think about how you spend that hour. Attending a five-hour "free" seminar during work hours suddenly doesn't seem so free, does it?

We often overlook the true value of our time, but considering its financial worth forces us to be more intentional. Before committing to something—whether it's a work project, social event, or personal activity—ask yourself: *Is this the best use of my time?* Being mindful of the value of your time empowers you to make choices that align with your goals.

One of the most powerful time-management tools is learning to say no. Every commitment you take on costs time, so make sure it's worth the investment.

"The secret to a productive life isn't more time, but better choices with the time you have."

– Author

Who Wants Your Time vs. Who Needs Your Time: My Digital Detox Journey

A few years ago, I attended a productivity seminar that, for the most part, covered familiar ground—goal setting, time management, and focus strategies. But there was one statement that hit me like a lightning bolt: *"We must learn to distinguish between who wants your time and who needs your time."*

At that moment, I realised how much of my time was being consumed by things that only wanted it but didn't need it. Like many of us, I had fallen into the trap of constantly checking my phone—emails, social media, notifications. What started as a quick glance at Facebook or Instagram would spiral into hours of scrolling. By the end of the day, I'd feel drained, but without any meaningful accomplishment.

What I hadn't realised was this: social media apps like Facebook, Instagram, and YouTube may seem "free," but they aren't. The real cost is your time—time you pay with every minute spent scrolling. These apps need your time because that's how they make money, by showing you ads. You are the product. The longer they keep you on the platform, the more they profit from your attention. What's worse, they fill your mind with distractions, pulling you away from what truly matters.

The same principle applies to relationships. We all have that needy friend who only calls or meets when they want something—perhaps to dump their emotional drama or relieve their boredom. These people only want your time, but do they deserve it? Are they adding value to your life, or are they merely siphoning off your energy?

I had my wake-up moment one evening when my wife was excitedly telling me about her day, and I was half-listening, mindlessly scrolling through Instagram. It hit me then—the real cost of my digital distractions. My family, my personal well-being, and the meaningful aspects of my work needed my time, but I was letting notifications, emails, and endless feeds steal it from them.

That seminar gave me the push I needed to take action, and I committed to a digital detox. I started small by turning off notifications, setting strict limits on social media usage, and dedicating specific "no-phone" hours to be fully present with my family. The change was immediate. I felt more connected, less stressed, and I was genuinely there for the people who needed me.

The digital detox wasn't just about reclaiming time—it helped me focus on what was truly important. I began to ask myself this life-changing question: *"Does this want my time, or does it need my time?"* This simple question became a filter for everything I did. It made me think twice before answering another call from someone who only reached out when they needed something or opening an app that didn't add value to my life.

Social media is designed to consume as much of your time as possible, keeping you distracted from what's important. But time is our most precious resource, and every minute we give to these distractions is a minute we take away from things that truly matter—like our family, personal development, or meaningful work.

This journey transformed my life. I learned to protect my time by identifying what truly needed it and letting go of everything that just wanted it. The clarity this brought allowed me to be more productive, more fulfilled, and more present for the people who mattered most.

So the next time you're tempted to spend hours scrolling through Instagram or take a call from that friend who only shows up with their emotional baggage, ask yourself: *Who or what really deserves my time?* This simple question can help you reclaim your time, your focus, and your life, just like it did for me.

"Time is the scarcest resource, and unless it is managed, nothing else can be managed."

– Peter Drucker

Ask Yourself

1. What are your top priorities and goals?
2. How can you create a structured schedule that aligns with your priorities?
3. What tasks can you delegate to free up time for more meaningful activities?

Time to Take Action

1. **Priority Assessment**: Reflect on your current tasks and goals. Write down what's most important to you. Use this list to guide your daily decisions.

2. **Time Blocking Plan**: Allocate specific time blocks for different activities throughout the day. Dedicate focused time to each task, minimising distractions during these periods.

   Example: You might block out 9-11 a.m. for focused work, 1-1:30 p.m. for emails, and 2-2.45 p.m. for lunch and a short walk. By creating specific time slots, you ensure that each task gets your full attention without overlap.

Final Thoughts

Mastering time management isn't about controlling time—it's about controlling how you use it. By setting priorities, creating a structured schedule, setting clear goals, blocking out time for important tasks, and being mindful of distractions, you can reclaim your time and live a more productive, fulfilling life. Remember, each moment is an opportunity. Use your time wisely, and watch your life transform in extraordinary ways.

Chapter 14

THE IMPORTANCE OF AUDIT AND REVIEW

"What gets measured gets managed."

– Peter Drucker

The Power of Regular Reflection

Auditing and reviewing your progress is a cornerstone of success. Superheroes constantly reflect on their missions, assess their performance, and make adjustments to improve. In much the same way, we need regular check-ins to assess our progress towards our personal and professional goals. By reviewing our achievements and setbacks, we can realign our efforts and move closer to our objectives.

Be Your Own Superhero: Embracing Audit and Review

To be your own superhero, you must integrate regular audits and reviews into your routine. This practice involves setting aside time to evaluate your progress, reflect on your achievements, and make necessary adjustments. By doing so, you ensure that you remain focused on your goals and can continually grow and improve.

In my own journey, regularly reviewing my business strategies has been critical. When I first started my logistics business, I often felt overwhelmed by competing priorities. It wasn't until I began auditing my weekly goals that I realised I needed to shift focus and delegate more effectively. This simple practice of review and adjustment helped me scale the business faster than I'd imagined.

"True growth comes not just from action but from review. Your greatest insights arise when you pause to measure how far you've come."

– Author

A Lesson from the Basketball Court: My Personal Scoreboard

One day, as I was passing through a park, I noticed a group of boys casually playing basketball. It was a laid-back scene—they were shooting hoops, joking around, and taking it easy. No one was in a rush, and the game felt more like a way to pass the time. An hour later, when I passed by again, I was struck by how different the scene had become. The same boys were now running hard, shouting, and playing with full intensity. Their focus was sharp, and every shot, pass, and move was executed with purpose.

Curious, I approached a boy on the sidelines and asked what had changed. He pointed to the scoreboard and said, *"Earlier, they were playing for fun, but now they are playing to win."*

The presence of the scoreboard had completely transformed their approach. When there was no score being kept, they played without urgency or commitment. But the moment their performance was tracked, their energy, drive, and effort skyrocketed. They were no longer playing just for fun—they were playing to win.

That moment stayed with me long after I left the park. It made me realise that in many aspects of my life—whether it was in my health, business, or personal growth—I was living without a scoreboard. Sure, I was working hard, but without a clear way to measure my progress, I was like those boys playing casually. I wasn't pushing myself to the fullest.

This realization led to a transformative change in how I approached life. I decided to create a scorecard for different aspects of my life, just as the boys had on the basketball court. Whether it was my health, business, or personal goals, I started tracking my progress. I set tangible milestones for my business, monitored my fitness goals, and kept a closer eye on my personal development.

In business, I began keeping a detailed scorecard for everything from revenue growth to customer satisfaction. It wasn't just about looking at the big picture anymore—I started breaking down my goals into measurable actions, ensuring I had a clear sense of where I stood and what needed improvement. This clarity gave me a new level of focus and motivation. It wasn't enough just to *work* hard anymore—I needed to *win*.

The same applied to my health. Instead of just exercising sporadically, I kept track of my workouts, measured my progress, and set specific goals. Having that personal scoreboard for my health changed everything. I became more disciplined, more consistent, and more intentional about my fitness.

This simple shift—having a scoreboard—was a game-changer. It taught me that measuring progress brings accountability and urgency. Without it, it's easy to coast through life, assuming you're making progress when, in reality, you're just going through the motions.

Tracking my progress in all aspects of my life helped me play *my* game with purpose and intensity, just like those boys on the basketball court. Every day, I'm reminded of the power of having a scorecard—it's not about perfection, but about knowing where you stand, adjusting, and striving to do better.

So, ask yourself: Do you have a scoreboard for your goals? If not, it might be time to put one in place and start playing to win.

The Importance of Having a "Scoreboard"

Without measurable goals or a way to track progress, it's easy to become complacent. Having a "scoreboard"—whether in the form of business metrics, fitness goals, or personal milestones—gives you something to strive for and a reason to push yourself beyond your comfort zone.

By setting clear goals and regularly reviewing my progress, I was able to stay ahead in a highly competitive industry. The same principle applies in our personal lives. By tracking our progress, we can recognise what's working, identify areas for improvement, and stay motivated to continue growing.

"The journey to greatness is paved with adjustments. Review, refine, and rise stronger after every reflection."

– Author

The Science Behind Audit and Review

Research shows that regularly reviewing goals significantly enhances personal and professional growth. A study in the *Journal of Applied Psychology* found that people who consistently reflect on their progress are more likely to achieve their goals. Another study by the *American Psychological Association* confirmed that regular reflection boosts performance and well-being by helping people stay focused and accountable.

Navigating the Roadblocks of Life: The Importance of Audit and Review

Imagine you're on a road trip from Delhi to Jaipur. You've meticulously mapped out your route, estimated your travel time, and set off with a sense of certainty. But, as often happens in life, the unexpected occurs. You encounter road construction, a missed turn, or maybe even an unplanned detour. What do you do in that moment? Do you abandon the trip entirely? Of course not. Instead, you pull over, reassess the situation, consult your GPS, find an alternative route, and adjust your schedule accordingly.

This simple scenario illustrates a powerful truth about life: plans will change, and challenges will arise. The same way you would reorient yourself on a road trip, you must do the same when pursuing your goals. But here's the catch—just like a driver who keeps going straight without acknowledging the detour signs, we often fail to audit and review our progress. We get so caught up in the grind, pushing forward blindly, that we miss the chance to take a much easier, faster route that is right in front of us.

Without regular audits and reviews, we could still be stuck in traffic, inching along, when there's a clear detour available.

Life, like a road trip, rarely goes as planned. There will be setbacks—some expected, many not. But the key difference between those who successfully reach their destination and those who give up halfway lies in the ability to stop, assess, and adjust. Regularly auditing your progress is like checking your GPS. It ensures you're still on the right path, but more importantly, it allows you to recalibrate when you're not.

Without this process, we risk drifting off course without even realizing it. You may continue to invest time and energy into a project, only to find that you're heading in the wrong direction, or worse, stuck in a loop, repeating the same mistakes. Without periodic reviews, you could be wasting valuable time and resources, driving further away from your intended destination when a simple shift in approach would have gotten you there faster and more efficiently.

In fact, life's "detours" often reveal opportunities we never would have considered otherwise. For example, a setback at work may prompt you to explore a different strategy, leading to greater success. Or a personal challenge could teach you a valuable lesson in resilience and adaptability, traits that become crucial as you continue on your journey. These moments of reflection and reassessment aren't just about getting back on track—they are about discovering new routes to success that may be even more rewarding than the original plan.

But here's where most of us falter: in our drive to achieve our goals, we forget the importance of regularly pausing to reflect. We push forward, assuming that more effort will get us there faster. And while hard work is essential, it's like pressing down on the gas pedal while heading in the wrong direction—it won't get you where you want to go any faster. In fact, it only takes you further away.

Auditing and reviewing your progress gives you the clarity you need to pivot when necessary. It's about checking in on your goals, evaluating what's working and what's not, and giving yourself permission to change course. It's a reminder that it's not the speed at which you move but the direction in which you're headed that matters most.

So, the next time you find yourself caught up in the hustle of life, remember to stop and ask yourself: Am I still on the right path? Are my actions aligned with my goals, or is it time to adjust my route? Just as a road trip with no checkpoints would likely result in missed turns and lost time, moving through life without regular audits can leave you stuck in the same place, even as you believe you're making progress.

Ultimately, the power of an audit and review isn't just about finding a way around roadblocks—it's about ensuring that every step you take is purposeful, efficient, and aligned with your destination. Without it, you may keep moving but never truly arrive.

Key Components of Effective Audit and Review

1. **Setting Clear Objectives**: Define specific, measurable goals that will guide your audit and review process. Clear objectives make it easier to evaluate progress and identify where you need to improve.
2. **Regular Scheduling**: Establish a regular review schedule—whether weekly, monthly, or quarterly. Consistency ensures you stay accountable and can make timely adjustments.
3. **Reflecting on Progress**: Take time to assess both your successes and areas for improvement. Honest reflection fuels growth.
4. **Analysing Data and Feedback**: Gather feedback from others, and review data related to your goals. This gives you an accurate picture of your progress and what you can do better.

5. **Making Adjustments**: After reviewing your progress, make necessary changes to your approach. Whether it's tweaking your strategy or resetting a goal, the real value of an audit lies in the adjustments you make moving forward.

"We all need people who will give us feedback. That's how we improve."

– Bill Gates

Ask Yourself

1. What are your current goals, and how clear are they?
2. How often do you review your progress, and what insights have you gained from these reviews?
3. What adjustments can you make today to better align your actions with your goals?

Time to Take Action

1. **Feedback Request**: Seek feedback from a trusted mentor or colleague on a specific area where you want to improve. Use this feedback to refine your approach.

2. **Tip:** Before seeking feedback, identify 2-3 specific areas where you want input. Clear, focused questions will lead to more constructive and actionable advice.

3. **Adjustment Action Plan**: After each review, note at least one adjustment you'll make based on the insights you've gathered. Set a timeline for implementing this change and stick to it.

   Example: If you've been consistently exercising for 30 minutes daily but not seeing the weight loss progress you expected, you decide to review your routine and realise that you haven't been tracking your diet. You decide to daily monitor your calorie intake.

Final Thoughts

Regularly auditing and reviewing your progress is a fundamental step in becoming your own superhero. By setting clear objectives, consistently evaluating your progress, and making the necessary adjustments, you can stay aligned with your goals and continue growing. Like the boys on the basketball court, using a "scoreboard" helps ensure that you're playing to win and constantly improving in your personal and professional life.

Section 6

Productivity and Proactivity

Chapter 15

OVERCOMING PROCRASTINATION

"The secret of getting ahead is getting started. The secret of getting started is breaking your complex overwhelming tasks into small manageable tasks, and then starting on the first one."

– Mark Twain

The Procrastination Trap

Procrastination—the act of delaying or postponing tasks—ensnares us all at some point. It's the silent thief of productivity, sneaking in when we least expect it, derailing our momentum and adding unnecessary stress to our lives. Whether it's that looming deadline, a difficult conversation, or a new project, procrastination creeps in and convinces us to wait "just a little longer." Even superheroes face moments of hesitation. They often struggle with taking decisive action at critical moments, but they also learn how to overcome it and leap into action. Likewise, for us, learning to combat procrastination is essential if we want to move forward in life and accomplish our goals. Understanding why we procrastinate, along with adopting proven strategies to break free from its grip, can transform our productivity and our lives.

"Procrastination is the shadow that blocks the light of progress. Defeat it by taking the first step."

– Author

Be Your Own Superhero: Conquering Procrastination

To unlock your inner superhero, you must first conquer procrastination. It's not just about checking things off a to-do list, but about reclaiming your time, energy, and focus. The key to defeating procrastination is self-awareness: recognizing when and why it occurs, identifying the underlying reasons for putting off tasks, and developing the mental tools to push through that resistance. By confronting procrastination head-on, you can gain control of your time, boost your productivity, and reach your goals more efficiently.

Procrastination as the Villain

Procrastination is much like a cunning villain in a superhero story—sneaky, persistent, and skilled at disguising itself as comfort or harmless delay. It seduces you with distractions, convincing you that tomorrow will be a better day to take action. It robs you of time, energy, and opportunity, making you feel powerless. But just like a superhero must learn to face and defeat their nemesis, you too have the power to conquer procrastination.

1. Identify the Villain:

The first step is to recognise procrastination when it strikes. Like any villain, procrastination uses tactics like fear, doubt, and distraction to hold you back. When you catch yourself avoiding tasks, ask: "What is this villain telling me?" Once you see procrastination for what it is, you can begin to fight back.

2. Use Your Superpowers:

Every superhero has unique abilities they can call upon to defeat their enemies. Your superpowers against procrastination are focus, discipline, and resilience. With tools like the Pomodoro Technique, the Two-Minute Rule, and time-blocking, you can fend off procrastination's attacks and stay on course toward your goals.

3. Make Action Your Superhero Move:

Just as superheroes must act decisively in the face of danger, you must take bold steps to defeat procrastination. Action is the ultimate weapon. Every time you choose to take a step forward, no matter how small, you weaken procrastination's hold on you and reclaim control of your time and energy.

The Science Behind Procrastination

Procrastination is a deeply ingrained psychological behavior. Research shows that it stems from multiple factors, including fear of failure, perfectionism, and even emotional regulation issues. A study published in *Psychological Science* explains that procrastination is a form of poor self-regulation, closely related to impulsivity. People often give in to immediate gratification (like watching a show or scrolling through social media) rather than focusing on the long-term benefits of completing a task. Another study conducted by the *American Psychological Association* highlights how procrastination contributes to heightened stress, anxiety, and overall dissatisfaction. It's not just a productivity issue—it's a well-being issue.

The Psychology of Procrastination

Procrastination is more than just putting off a task; it is often deeply rooted in our psychology. Several factors contribute to why we procrastinate, including perfectionism, fear of failure, and feeling overwhelmed. Understanding these underlying causes can help us confront and overcome procrastination with greater awareness.

1. Perfectionism: The Pursuit of an Impossible Ideal

Perfectionism is one of the most common causes of procrastination. Perfectionists often delay starting tasks because they set unrealistically high standards for themselves. The fear of producing anything less than perfect can paralyze action. Instead of viewing tasks as opportunities to learn and grow, perfectionists feel that their work must be flawless from the start. This creates an overwhelming fear of making mistakes, leading to avoidance.

Example: Imagine you need to write a proposal for a new project. If you're a perfectionist, you might feel that unless the proposal is perfect, it's not worth submitting. As a result, you delay starting, fearing that your ideas won't be good enough. Days pass, and you continue to put it off, convincing yourself that you'll "start tomorrow" when you feel more prepared. In reality, you're using perfectionism as a shield against potential failure.

2. Fear of Failure: The Hidden Saboteur

The fear of failure is another major culprit behind procrastination. When we feel that a task carries a risk of failure, our mind tends to avoid it to protect us from the discomfort of failure. This fear can be especially prevalent in situations where the stakes are high, such as job interviews, major presentations, or starting a new business venture. The irony is that avoiding these tasks due to fear only increases the likelihood of failure in the long run.

Example: You have a job interview for a dream role, but instead of preparing, you find yourself cleaning your house, scrolling through social media, or doing any number of low-priority tasks. The root of this procrastination is fear—fear that you won't perform well in the interview, that you won't be the best candidate, or that you'll be rejected. By procrastinating, you protect yourself from confronting these potential outcomes, but at the cost of missing the chance to succeed.

3. Feeling Overwhelmed: The Weight of Too Much

When faced with a large or complex task, many people feel overwhelmed by its size and scope. This feeling can lead to paralysis, where starting seems too daunting. Procrastination becomes a coping mechanism to avoid the discomfort of uncertainty and stress. However, this only compounds the problem, as the task remains incomplete, leading to even more anxiety.

Example: You have a 50-page report to finish by the end of the month, and the thought of it feels monumental. Rather than breaking it down into smaller, manageable sections, you continue to procrastinate, waiting for a moment when you feel "ready" to tackle the whole thing. Each day you delay, the report looms larger in your mind, intensifying your anxiety and further preventing you from starting.

"When you confront procrastination, you're not just defeating a bad habit—you're reclaiming your time, your energy, and your potential."

– Author

"Eat That Frog" – A Game-Changing Approach

One of the most transformative approaches to overcoming procrastination is found in Brian Tracy's book, *Eat That Frog!*. The premise is simple: every day, identify the hardest, most important task—your "frog"—and complete it first thing in the morning. The idea is that if you tackle your biggest challenge right away, the rest of your day will feel easier by comparison.

This philosophy hit home for me. Like many, I used to start my day with smaller, easier tasks—emails, quick errands, administrative work—thinking that by getting these out of the way, I'd be ready for the bigger challenges. But what I found was that by the time I got to the important tasks, I was mentally drained. My energy had been spent on trivial things. When I adopted the "Eat That Frog" mentality, everything changed. My productivity soared. By getting the toughest job done first, I not only felt accomplished, but my entire day became more efficient.

The "Eat That Frog" technique forces you to confront the task you're most likely to procrastinate on. By attacking it first, you build momentum, making the rest of your workday more productive. It's an incredibly effective strategy for anyone who struggles with getting started.

Real-Life Example: J.K. Rowling's Writing Struggles

Even high-achievers like J.K. Rowling, the celebrated author of the *Harry Potter* series, have struggled with procrastination. Before she became one of the most successful authors in history, Rowling faced significant challenges. While she had the idea for *Harry Potter* in her mind, she often found herself procrastinating. She was raising a child as a single mother, living on welfare, and dealing with the pressure of creating something worthwhile.

Rowling has spoken openly about how she dealt with self-doubt and the fear of failing at what she loved most—writing. She realised that the fear of not being good enough was at the root of her procrastination. It was only when she broke her writing down into manageable steps—one chapter, one character at a time—that she began making progress. By focusing on small, achievable goals, Rowling slowly but steadily brought the magical world of *Harry Potter* to life.

Her story illustrates that procrastination can be overcome with deliberate action and a structured approach. Today, her success is a testament to the power of taking those first small steps, no matter how daunting the larger goal may seem.

Ask Yourself: *If J.K. Rowling could overcome procrastination and self-doubt to create one of the most beloved book series in history, what's stopping you from taking the first step toward your own goals?*

The Value of Breaking Tasks Down

Often, procrastination is a result of feeling overwhelmed by the sheer size or complexity of a task. When a project feels too big, it's tempting to avoid it altogether. This is where breaking tasks into smaller, more manageable steps can be a game-changer. The idea is simple: start small, and build momentum.

For example, if you need to write a report, don't think of it as a single daunting task. Instead, break it down into steps—research, outlining, drafting, and editing. By focusing on completing just one step at a time, you'll feel a sense of accomplishment and keep moving forward. Before you know it, the report will be finished.

Key Components of Overcoming Procrastination

1. **Understanding Procrastination**: Identifying why you procrastinate is critical. Often, it's linked to deeper psychological reasons, such as fear of failure, perfectionism, or feeling overwhelmed. Recognizing the root cause will help you address it directly.

2. **Breaking Tasks into Smaller Steps**: Large tasks can feel paralyzing, which makes starting seem impossible. Breaking them down into smaller, manageable steps reduces this feeling of overwhelm and makes it easier to take that crucial first step.
3. **Setting Clear Goals and Deadlines**: Procrastination often thrives in the absence of structure. Establishing specific, measurable goals with deadlines provides the framework needed to combat it.
4. **Creating a Productive Environment**: A cluttered or distracting workspace can reinforce procrastination. Optimize your environment to foster focus and productivity—this could mean decluttering, limiting distractions, or setting up a space that energizes you.
5. **Using Time Management Techniques**: Adopting methods like time-blocking or the Pomodoro Technique ensures that your time is structured and dedicated to focused work, making procrastination less likely to creep in.

Personal Story of Overcoming Procrastination

A few years ago, my business had reached a frustrating plateau. Sales were stagnant, innovation was lacking, and operational inefficiencies were eating into profits. Despite long working hours, I couldn't pinpoint why the business wasn't growing. Stress was mounting, and I realised that I needed an outside perspective. I sought out a business consultant.

During our first meeting, the consultant asked me a single, pivotal question: "Who is your CGO?" I had no idea what he meant. "Your Chief Growth Officer," he clarified. "Who's responsible for driving growth in your company?"

As a small business owner, I didn't have the resources for such roles. I explained that I handled growth myself, but his next question hit hard: "Are you actually acting like your company's CGO?"

That question changed everything for me. When I reflected on my daily routine, I realised that much of my time was consumed by operational tasks—emails, meetings, troubleshooting minor issues—none of which contributed to the business's growth. I was procrastinating on the hard work of strategizing, client outreach, and innovation. I avoided these growth-driving activities because they were uncomfortable and involved risk.

From that point forward, I shifted my priorities. Every day, I focused on the tasks that would drive business growth. I implemented a 5-3-1 technique to make growth a priority:

- I committed to making 5 phone calls to new prospective clients every day.
- I arranged 3 client meetings each week to build relationships and explore new opportunities.
- Once a month, I focused on implementing 1 new innovative customer delight practice to surprise and engage my existing clients, ensuring they felt valued.

This structured approach kept me accountable and helped push the business forward in a tangible, focused way. I also shifted my priorities overall—every day, I concentrated on the tasks that would drive business growth. The results were transformational—sales increased, profits grew, and I felt more in control of the company's future.

Procrastination wasn't just delaying my productivity; it was delaying my company's success. Overcoming it required acknowledging my avoidance behaviors and taking bold, deliberate action.

"Procrastination is opportunity's assassin."

– Victor Kiam

Ask Yourself

1. What are the main reasons behind your procrastination—fear, perfectionism, or feeling overwhelmed?
2. How can breaking tasks into smaller steps help you overcome procrastination and start moving toward your goals?

3. What time management techniques could you implement today to reduce distractions and stay focused?

Time to Take Action

1. **Pomodoro Technique**: Set a timer for 25 minutes, work intensely on a task, and then take a 5-minute break. After four "Pomodoros," take a longer break.

   Why it helps: This method breaks tasks into manageable time intervals, making it easier to start and maintain focus without feeling overwhelmed.

2. **Two-Minute Rule**: If a task can be done in two minutes or less, do it immediately. For larger tasks, commit to starting for just two minutes—this often builds momentum to keep going.

   Why it helps: Tackling small tasks immediately and overcoming resistance to starting larger tasks eliminates the risk of tasks piling up.

3. **Eat That Frog**: Each morning, identify your "frog"—the most difficult and important task—and complete it first thing.

   Why it helps: Accomplishing your hardest task early frees up mental energy for the rest of the day, making you more productive.

4. **Time Blocking**: Dedicate specific blocks of time to different tasks, focusing solely on one task during each block.

   Why it helps: This creates structure and reduces multitasking, improving focus and productivity.

5. **The 5-Second Rule**: When you feel the urge to procrastinate, count down from 5 to 1 and take immediate action.

   Why it helps: This rule interrupts the hesitation loop and propels you into immediate action, bypassing procrastination.

Final Thoughts

Overcoming procrastination is a vital step in becoming your own superhero. By understanding its causes, breaking tasks into smaller, actionable steps, creating a productive environment, and implementing proven time management techniques, you can conquer procrastination and unlock your full potential. Productivity isn't just about getting things done—it's about getting the right things done. Take the leap, tackle the hardest tasks, and move closer to the life and goals you envision for yourself.

Chapter 16

DEVELOPING SYSTEMS FOR SUCCESS

"You do not rise to the level of your goals. You fall to the level of your systems."

– James Clear, *Atomic Habits*

The Power of Systems

While setting goals is essential, achieving them consistently depends on the systems you have in place. Superheroes don't just rely on their powers; they create systems to monitor crime, manage resources, and even maintain their secret identities. Without these systems, even the most powerful heroes would struggle to stay organised and effective. The same principle applies to us. Systems allow us to handle the complexities of daily life with efficiency, reduce decision fatigue, and ensure progress toward our goals in a sustainable way.

Systems are structured processes, routines, and frameworks that help you manage tasks, minimize errors, and improve performance over time. By creating systems, you remove the need to constantly reinvent the wheel. Systems ensure that progress is not accidental but consistent, giving you a reliable path to success. They are the foundation for long-term productivity and well-being.

"A strong system turns ordinary effort into extraordinary results."

– Author

Be Your Own Superhero: Embracing Systems

To be your own superhero, you must develop and embrace systems that make your life easier and more productive. Systems allow you to achieve more with less effort, maintain consistency, and make better decisions. When you have effective systems in place, you create a process that operates almost on autopilot—saving time, reducing stress, and freeing up mental energy to focus on the big picture.

In today's world, **AI has emerged as a new superpower** available to each one of us, transforming the way we approach productivity and success. Just as superheroes rely on cutting-edge tools to enhance their abilities, we now have access to artificial intelligence that can automate tasks, analyze data, and streamline processes with incredible speed and accuracy. AI helps us manage information overload, make smarter decisions, and free up valuable time for creative and strategic thinking. Whether it's using AI-powered scheduling apps, data analytics, or virtual assistants, this technology empowers us to operate at peak efficiency, making the impossible seem possible. When integrated into our systems, AI becomes a powerful ally in achieving our goals faster and with less effort, giving us an edge in the rapidly evolving landscape of work and life.

The Science Behind Systems

Research has shown that effective systems significantly boost productivity and help people achieve their goals. In a study published in *Organizational Behavior and Human Decision Processes*, participants who used structured routines were 50% more likely to reach their objectives compared to those without established systems. Structured systems reduce cognitive overload by automating certain processes, freeing up brain power for more critical tasks. Another study by the *American Psychological Association* found that systems reduce decision fatigue and increase overall well-being, as they create predictability in an otherwise chaotic world.

Why Systems Matter More Than Goals

There's a common misconception that setting ambitious goals is the key to success. While goals are important, systems are what actually drive progress. Think of it this way: a goal is your destination, but your system is the map that will get you there. You may have a goal to lose weight, but without a system that includes regular exercise, meal planning, and accountability, the goal will remain elusive.

If your goal is to write a book, the system is writing 500 words every day at a designated time. If your goal is to grow your business, the system is making consistent outreach to new clients, managing projects efficiently, and reviewing your performance regularly. Systems are the step-by-step processes that ensure you are consistently working towards your goal without relying on bursts of motivation.

Without systems, even the clearest goals can become distant dreams. Imagine you're trying to climb a mountain—your goal is the summit. Without a system of step-by-step actions—like training, gathering the right gear, and following a clear path—you're likely to lose your way. Systems ensure that you keep moving forward, one step at a time, until the summit is reached.

System Flexibility

Just as superheroes must adapt to new villains and evolving threats, your systems must also evolve. Flexibility in your systems ensures you don't become rigid or stuck when circumstances change. For instance, if your goal shifts from running a marathon to recovering from an injury, your system needs to adjust accordingly. Regularly assessing your system's effectiveness is crucial—after all, even the most powerful system can become outdated over time.

"When you rely on systems, progress is no longer accidental. It's inevitable."

– Author

Practical Case Study: Toyota's Kaizen Philosophy

Toyota's legendary success is largely due to its implementation of the Kaizen philosophy, which emphasises continuous improvement. Instead of focusing on massive leaps in performance, Toyota has built a culture around refining small systems and processes. Every employee is encouraged to look for ways to improve workflows, reduce waste, and increase efficiency.

This incremental, system-driven approach allows Toyota to maintain high levels of quality and innovation. The company's success isn't due to massive overhauls or occasional bursts of brilliance—it's due to the consistent refinement of systems that allows the company to make steady, ongoing improvements.

Just like Toyota, we can implement small, consistent improvements in our personal and professional systems. The Kaizen mindset encourages constant refinement, ensuring our systems evolve as our needs change and our goals shift.

Ask Yourself: *If Toyota could achieve global success by developing effective systems and embracing continuous improvement through small, consistent changes, what's stopping you from applying the same approach to improve your own life or work?*

Key Components of Effective Systems

1. **Goal Setting**: Systems should be designed with specific objectives in mind. Break your goals down into actionable steps and create systems that allow you to work toward these steps consistently.
2. **Routine and Consistency**: Establish routines that support your goals. Consistency is what turns good intentions into lasting habits.
3. **Automation**: Where possible, automate repetitive tasks. Automation tools—such as scheduling apps, task management software, and automated emails—save time and reduce human error.
4. **Monitoring and Feedback**: Systems must be flexible and adaptable. Regularly monitor the effectiveness of your system by collecting

feedback, whether through data, personal reflection, or input from others.

5. **Flexibility and Adaptability**: Systems should evolve as your needs and goals change. Periodically reassess and tweak your processes to ensure they continue to serve you effectively.

Personal Story: The Power of Systems in Action

"People don't work, systems do." This principle has profoundly shaped my approach to success. Let me share an experiment I conducted at home to illustrate this idea.

One day, I told my wife I needed to leave for work an hour earlier than usual for the next two weeks. Everything had to run smoothly: breakfast ready, lunch packed, and me out the door by 9 AM. What my wife didn't know was that this was part of an experiment—one that tested how long individual effort alone could sustain this new routine.

At first, things went well. But as the days progressed, small delays started creeping in. One morning, breakfast was late; another day, the lunch wasn't packed on time. Despite my wife's best efforts, cracks began to appear, and the routine started to falter.

Why did this happen? Because the success of the routine was based solely on individual effort, without a reliable system in place. Compare this to a hotel or hospital, where breakfast is served at 7:00 AM sharp, day after day, no matter the circumstances. The secret behind their precision? They don't rely on individual effort alone—they rely on well-established systems.

A system doesn't depend on one person's memory, mood, or energy level. It's designed to function independently of the human element, ensuring the desired outcome is achieved consistently, even in the face of unforeseen challenges.

Whether in business or at home, systems allow us to manage tasks efficiently, eliminate human error, and free up mental energy for more important decisions. Systems create consistency, reduce stress, and help you focus on the tasks that truly matter.

Implementing Systems in My Business

This lesson resonated deeply with me, and I knew I had to bring it into my business. I started by designing and implementing systems for every major task within the company, from handling client complaints to introducing new clients into the system. Each process was documented, streamlined, and automated where possible. It allowed my team to follow structured guidelines, reducing errors and ensuring consistency across the board.

For example, when a new client joined, there was now a clear, repeatable system for onboarding. From gathering the necessary documents, assigning account managers, and sending out welcome emails, the process ran like clockwork—without me having to intervene at every stage.

Another major area I reformed was client follow-ups for outstanding dues. Rather than relying on memory or sporadic reminders, I set up a clear system with automated reminders that triggered emails or calls at the right times, ensuring no payment was overlooked. My team could now manage receivables efficiently, freeing up their time to focus on other tasks.

Additionally, handling client complaints became far more systematic. Rather than dealing with each issue as it came up and potentially letting some fall through the cracks, I put a system in place. A dedicated support team was created to handle inquiries, track complaints, and ensure resolution within a defined period. This system gave our clients the confidence that their concerns would be addressed professionally and promptly.

Developing and implementing these systems not only streamlined operations but also freed up my time. No longer bogged down by routine tasks or micromanaging my team, I was able to focus on starting new business ventures and chasing my passions, whether that was pursuing creative projects or spending more quality time with my family.

As a result, my business saw steady growth—sales climbed, efficiency improved, and client satisfaction rose. My team was empowered to handle tasks independently, allowing me to work on the business rather than being trapped working in the business.

Systems are the backbone of any successful enterprise. Without them, you're left constantly putting out fires. With them, you're free to focus on innovation, expansion, and building a future that aligns with your vision.

Famous Quote

"A bad system will beat a good person every time."

– W. Edwards Deming

Ask Yourself

1. What are your top three goals, and how can systems help you achieve them?
2. What recurring tasks in your daily routine could be automated to save time and reduce mental load?
3. How often do you review your systems to ensure they are working effectively?

Time to Take Action

1. **System Design**: Choose one of your major goals and design a system around it. Outline the steps, tools, and routines that will help you achieve consistent progress toward that goal.

   Example: You set a goal to lose 10kg in 6 months. Your system design will include creating a workout schedule (e.g., 3 days of strength training, 2 days of cardio), planning meals in advance on Sundays and tracking daily food intake using a calorie-counting app with weekly check-ins for progress.

2. **Automation Assessment**: Look at your current daily or weekly tasks. Identify at least three tasks that could be automated using technology (e.g., calendar scheduling, email filters, automated billing).

Final Thoughts

Developing systems for success is not just a productivity hack—it's a way of life. By building systems that align with your goals, automating repetitive tasks, and consistently refining your processes, you create a structure that supports your long-term success. Systems allow you to focus on what matters most, reduce stress, and achieve more with less effort.

In the end, it's not about working harder—it's about working smarter. Let systems do the heavy lifting for you, and watch as you steadily progress toward your goals, one structured step at a time.

Chapter 17

RESPONDING VS. REACTING TO SITUATIONS

"Between stimulus and response, there is a space. In that space is our power to choose our response. In our response lies our growth and our freedom."

– Viktor Frankl

The Importance of Response Over Reaction

In life, situations arise that demand our attention and action—sometimes urgently. Just like superheroes who maintain their cool during crises, we too must learn the art of responding rather than reacting. The difference between the two lies in emotional control, thoughtful decision-making, and composure. Responding requires us to pause, assess, and choose our actions consciously, while reacting is often impulsive, driven by emotions like fear or anger.

Reacting can escalate situations unnecessarily, leaving us with regret or unresolved problems. On the other hand, responding leads to better decision-making, improved relationships, and personal growth. Mastering this skill is not only crucial for handling life's challenges with grace but also for enhancing emotional intelligence.

Emotional triggers, such as feeling disrespected, overwhelmed, or criticized, often ignite knee-jerk reactions. By identifying these triggers, you can create space between the event and your response. For example, if criticism tends to trigger defensiveness, recognizing this in yourself allows you to pause and approach feedback more constructively.

"Your strength lies not in your power to act, but in your power to pause."

– Author

Be Your Own Superhero: Mastering the Art of Response

Superheroes aren't just celebrated for their strength—they are admired for their ability to remain calm and collected under pressure. They don't rush into action; they think through their next move, ensuring that their decisions align with their mission. To be your own superhero, you need to cultivate the ability to respond thoughtfully rather than react impulsively.

This process begins with self-awareness, knowing your emotional triggers, and developing emotional regulation strategies. Responding involves taking control of your reactions, allowing you to handle challenges with clarity and wisdom.

The Science Behind Responding vs. Reacting

Scientific research supports the profound benefits of learning to respond rather than react. A study published in the *Journal of Personality and Social Psychology* found that individuals who respond to situations with mindfulness and emotional regulation experience lower levels of stress and anxiety, and higher emotional resilience. These individuals are also more likely to make sound decisions under pressure, fostering better relationships and overall well-being.

Another study from the *American Psychological Association* highlights how mindfulness-based practices help people regulate their emotional responses, especially in difficult situations. Mindful individuals are able to pause, reflect, and make choices that lead to better outcomes, rather than being driven by emotional impulses.

Story: The Waiter and the Cockroach

Here's a story that illustrates the clear distinction between reacting and responding, and how these two approaches can dramatically alter the outcome of any situation.

One afternoon, a group of women were enjoying their lunch at a restaurant. As they chatted, one of the women noticed a cockroach crawling on the floor near their table. Startled and horrified, she screamed, jumping onto her chair in a panic. Her friends quickly followed suit, creating a scene of chaos—plates crashed to the floor, drinks spilled, and the women's shrieks filled the room.

In the middle of this commotion, a waiter calmly approached the table, noticed the source of the panic, and without a hint of hesitation, picked up the cockroach with a napkin. He carried it outside and disposed of it. The panic immediately subsided, and the restaurant returned to normal.

The situation was the same for both the women and the waiter—a cockroach had entered their space. The women reacted impulsively, making the situation worse. The waiter, however, responded thoughtfully and calmly, diffusing the chaos. This story shows us that while we cannot always control what happens to us, we can control how we choose to respond.

The waiter's calm response wasn't an accident; it likely came from a practiced system of emotional regulation. Just like in any skill, the ability to respond thoughtfully improves with practice, such as mindfulness techniques or self-reflection.

"Mastering the pause between emotion and action is where true personal growth begins."

– Author

Key Components of Responding vs. Reacting

1. **Self-Awareness**: The first step in learning to respond rather than react is recognizing your emotional triggers. When you're aware of what causes you to react impulsively, you can take proactive steps to manage those emotions.
2. **Emotional Regulation**: Developing emotional regulation techniques, such as deep breathing or mindfulness, can help you manage intense emotions in the moment. This practice helps you stay calm, allowing for thoughtful responses rather than knee-jerk reactions.
3. **Thoughtful Decision-Making**: A response is a result of pausing and evaluating the situation before acting. By taking time to think through your actions and their potential outcomes, you make wiser decisions that benefit you in the long run.
4. **Mindfulness Practices**: Regular mindfulness exercises, such as meditation or grounding techniques, keep you centered in the present. This practice minimizes distractions from overwhelming emotions and improves your ability to respond calmly in stressful situations.
5. **Effective Communication**: Thoughtful responses often involve clear and respectful communication. Learning to articulate your thoughts with composure allows you to foster healthier relationships and resolve conflicts more effectively.

"It's not what happens to you, but how you react to it that matters."

– Epictetus

How to Respond Instead of Reacting in Stressful Situations – My Personal Journey

I have always found it difficult to control my emotions, especially when confronted with a disrespectful or hurtful person. In those moments, my instinct was often to react—to match their hurtful words with anger or frustration. But over time, I realised something crucial: by reacting emotionally, I wasn't solving the situation. Instead, I was stooping to their level, escalating the conflict, and ultimately feeling worse.

But how do you stay calm in such situations, and more importantly, why should you?

For years, I wrestled with this question. Then one day, I stumbled upon a YouTube video by Gaur Gopal Das titled *"Don't React, Respond."* In this video, he presents a simple but profound analogy that completely changed my perspective. He places two sealed bottles in front of him: one filled with cola and the other with water. He explains that these bottles represent us, while the liquid inside symbolizes our emotional state.

First, he shakes the cola bottle vigorously, simulating the pressures and provocations we face—insults, disrespect, life's unexpected curveballs. When he opens the bottle, cola fizzes out violently, spraying everywhere, making a mess. Then, he shakes the water bottle just as vigorously. But when he opens it, nothing happens—the water remains calm and contained.

This is where the lesson hit me hard. Just like the cola and water bottles, our emotional state determines how we "open up" under stress. If we're in a "cola state," we're unstable, reactive, and when shaken by life, we explode and create a mess. But if we're in a "water state," we remain calm, grounded, and composed, no matter how much we're shaken.

The beauty of this analogy is that we have the power to choose which state we want to be in, regardless of the external provocations. I realised that responding, rather than reacting, wasn't about repressing emotions but mastering them. Staying calm, even in the face of insults or disrespect, gives you control over the situation. It allows you to rise above the emotional turbulence and maintain your dignity, peace, and sense of self-respect.

From that day forward, I made a conscious effort to be the "water bottle." When faced with stressful situations or disrespectful individuals, I pause, breathe, and choose how to respond—not react. It doesn't mean suppressing your feelings, but rather controlling them so that you can think clearly and act wisely.

The next time you're in a heated situation, remember: you can either let your emotions fizz out uncontrollably, or you can stay calm, collected, and in control. The choice is always yours.

Ask Yourself

1. What are some common triggers that cause you to react impulsively in your personal or professional life?
2. How can mindfulness and emotional regulation techniques help you improve your ability to respond thoughtfully?
3. In which areas of your life could better communication and thoughtful responses improve your relationships?

Time to Take Action

1. **Role-Playing**: Practice role-playing challenging situations with a friend or family member. Choose scenarios that are likely to trigger emotional reactions and focus on responding thoughtfully. This exercise will help you improve your emotional regulation and communication skills.

   Example: Imagine you've been working hard on a project at work, and during a team meeting, your boss criticizes your approach in front of everyone. Your natural instinct might be to react defensively, perhaps arguing or feeling hurt by the criticism. Instead of reacting, you can use this as a role-playing scenario to practice responding thoughtfully.

2. **The 5-Second Pause**: When faced with a situation that triggers an emotional reaction, practice pausing for five seconds before you respond. This brief pause gives you time to reflect and choose a response that aligns with your values and long-term goals.

Final Thoughts

Mastering the art of responding thoughtfully, rather than reacting impulsively, is essential for personal growth, better decision-making, and stronger relationships. By cultivating self-awareness, practicing emotional regulation, and learning to communicate effectively, you can transform how you handle life's challenges. The power to respond lies within you—and it is the key to becoming your own superhero.

Section 7

Gratitude and Growth

Chapter 18

THE POWER OF GRATITUDE

"Gratitude can transform common days into thanksgivings, turn routine jobs into joy, and change ordinary opportunities into blessings."

– William Arthur Ward

The Impact of Gratitude

Gratitude is a transformative force that has the power to shift your perspective and elevate your experience of life. Just as superheroes often draw strength and motivation from their gratitude for their abilities, allies, and the world they protect, practicing gratitude in our own lives can significantly enhance our mental, emotional, and physical well-being.

Gratitude is about more than saying "thank you" for the obvious. It's about training your mind to focus on the things you have, rather than dwelling on what you lack. In a world driven by comparisons and a constant pursuit of more, gratitude serves as a powerful anchor that grounds us in the present and helps us find contentment. It allows us to recognise the beauty in what we already possess and, in turn, attracts more positivity into our lives.

Be Your Own Superhero: Harnessing Gratitude

To be your own superhero, you must harness the power of gratitude. This means recognizing and appreciating even the smallest blessings in your life. When you consciously practice gratitude, you build resilience and unlock the ability to navigate life's challenges with a positive, empowered mindset. Gratitude enhances your mental clarity, emotional strength, and relationships, helping you become the best version of yourself.

Superheroes find purpose in what they have—whether it's their powers, allies, or the people they protect. Similarly, when we focus on the good in our lives, we draw upon a deep well of strength and inspiration. A grateful heart not only leads to personal growth but also opens up avenues for kindness, compassion, and collaboration with others.

The Science Behind Gratitude

The science of gratitude reveals that it's not just a feel-good practice—it has real, measurable benefits. Research by Dr. Robert Emmons, one of the foremost experts on the subject, found that people who regularly practice gratitude experience lower levels of stress and depression, better physical health, and higher levels of happiness.

Similarly, a study published in the *Journal of Positive Psychology* highlighted that gratitude enhances emotional well-being and fosters prosocial behavior. People who are grateful tend to be more helpful, compassionate, and connected to others. The act of counting blessings doesn't just make you feel good in the moment—it changes your brain chemistry, making it easier to focus on the positive and maintain a sense of fulfillment.

By practicing gratitude, we shift the brain's focus from stressors to blessings, making it easier to navigate difficulties and build resilience. In essence, gratitude rewires the brain to look for opportunities rather than obstacles.

Shifting from Scarcity to Abundance Mindset

Many of us are conditioned to focus on what we don't have—the next promotion, a bigger house, or a more exciting life. This mindset creates a sense of scarcity, making it difficult to feel fulfilled. Practicing gratitude shifts our focus from what is missing to what is already abundant in our lives. By embracing this shift, we stop chasing after happiness and instead recognise that happiness is already within reach. The more we acknowledge our blessings, the more we attract new opportunities and experiences that align with this abundance.

Social Impact of Gratitude

Gratitude doesn't just transform the individual; it spreads like ripples in a pond. When we express appreciation to others, we strengthen bonds, foster trust, and build stronger communities. Acts of gratitude have been shown to increase cooperation and create a positive feedback loop, where kindness and support flourish. In a world that often feels divided, gratitude serves as a unifying force that connects us through shared appreciation and empathy.

"When you practice gratitude, you harness the power to turn what you have into all you need."

– Author

My Thrust with Gratitude

A few years ago, I found myself feeling strangely dissatisfied. On the surface, I had everything—good health, a supportive family, a successful business, and great friends. Yet deep down, I felt something was missing. Despite my outward success, I felt an emptiness that I couldn't explain.

One day, I realised I had fallen into the trap of social media comparison. I was constantly scrolling through Instagram and Facebook, seeing snapshots of other people's seemingly perfect lives. Whether it was a friend's exotic vacation or a colleague's professional milestone, I started to feel like my life wasn't measuring up. I became obsessed with what I didn't have, despite my abundant blessings. The endless comparison slowly chipped away at my happiness, and soon, I found myself in a state of perpetual dissatisfaction.

One morning, I woke up with a moment of clarity. I realised that I had handed over my happiness to social media, and it was time to take it back. I deleted all social media apps from my phone and began to focus inward. Instead of scrolling through curated highlights, I began practicing gratitude by starting my mornings with quiet reflection, appreciating my family, my business, my health, and my home. The shift was immediate.

By reclaiming control over my mindset and focusing on gratitude, I rediscovered a sense of fulfillment. My relationships deepened, my stress levels decreased, and I found more joy in my day-to-day life. Gratitude grounded me and made me see that true happiness wasn't found in the endless pursuit of more, but in appreciating the beauty of what I already had.

Key Components of Practicing Gratitude

1. **Gratitude Journaling**: Writing down three things you are grateful for every day helps shift your focus from negativity to positivity. This simple act builds a habit of appreciation, rewiring your brain to look for the good in everyday life.
2. **Expressing Gratitude**: Taking time to thank others, whether through a kind word, a note, or a gesture, not only strengthens your relationships but also reinforces your own sense of abundance.
3. **Mindful Appreciation**: Engage in mindful moments of appreciation throughout the day. This could be as simple as savoring a warm cup of coffee, appreciating the sunlight, or recognizing the kindness of a stranger.
4. **Reflecting on Challenges**: Instead of resenting difficulties, view them as opportunities for growth. By reflecting on the lessons learned through tough times, you foster resilience and deepen your gratitude for the strength you've gained.

"Gratitude makes sense of our past, brings peace for today, and creates a vision for tomorrow."

– Melody Beattie

Case Study: The Secret and the Law of Attraction

It's impossible to talk about gratitude without mentioning *The Secret* by Rhonda Byrne. The book is based on the Law of Attraction, a powerful concept that suggests we attract what we focus on. Byrne's central message is that the act of practicing gratitude is key to manifesting the life you desire.

The Law of Attraction posits that when we focus on gratitude, we naturally attract more good things into our lives. It's a cycle—when we express gratitude for what we have, we raise our emotional frequency, making us more attuned to positive opportunities.

For many readers of *The Secret*, this mindset shift was revolutionary. People started applying gratitude in their daily lives, from acknowledging small blessings to showing deep appreciation for larger milestones. The results were astounding. Countless individuals shared stories of how practicing gratitude transformed their relationships, finances, and personal growth.

Gratitude isn't just about feeling good—it's about creating a vibration of abundance that opens doors to new possibilities. When you embrace gratitude, you invite success, happiness, and peace into your life.

Ask Yourself

1. What are three things you are grateful for today?
2. How has practicing gratitude positively impacted your relationships?
3. How can you incorporate gratitude into your daily routine to foster more positivity?

Time to Take Action

1. **Gratitude Meditation**: Take 10 minutes each day to focus on things you're grateful for. Close your eyes and visualize the people, experiences, and blessings in your life that bring you joy. This practice helps you build a mindset of abundance.

2. **Daily Gratitude Sharing**: At the end of each day, share one thing you are grateful for with a family member, friend, or colleague. Invite them to do the same. This not only spreads positivity but also reinforces your own gratitude practice.

Final Thoughts

Practicing gratitude is one of the most powerful steps you can take toward becoming your own superhero. By consistently recognizing and appreciating the good in your life, you will not only boost your well-being but also strengthen your relationships, increase resilience, and foster a positive mindset. Gratitude transforms ordinary moments into extraordinary experiences, reminding you that happiness lies in appreciating what you already have.

Chapter 19

CONTINUOUS LEARNING AND PERSONAL GROWTH

"Once you stop learning, you start dying."

– Albert Einstein

The Importance of Lifelong Learning

Lifelong learning is at the heart of personal growth and fulfilment. Much like superheroes who continually hone their abilities to face new challenges, we too must cultivate a mindset of constant learning. Embracing continuous learning equips us to adapt, evolve, and thrive in a world that is ever-changing. It keeps our minds sharp, expands our perspectives, and opens doors to new opportunities.

"True personal growth isn't about mastering what you already know—it's about daring to learn what you don't."

– Author

Be Your Own Superhero: Embracing Lifelong Learning

To unleash your inner superhero, you must commit to lifelong learning. This means nurturing curiosity, exploring new ideas, and seeking experiences that push you to grow. When you view life as a continuous learning journey, every challenge becomes an opportunity to gain knowledge, refine skills, and improve yourself.

Superheroes don't rely solely on innate powers; they train, adapt, and grow stronger with each experience. Similarly, lifelong learners don't rest on their past achievements—they seek new challenges and possibilities, always striving for personal and professional growth.

Remember, failure isn't the end—it's an essential part of learning. Just like superheroes learn from each battle, you can turn mistakes into opportunities for growth.

The Science Behind Lifelong Learning

Research underscores the immense benefits of continuous learning for both cognitive and emotional health. A study published in *Psychological Science* found that engaging in intellectually stimulating activities enhances cognitive function, slowing age-related decline. Meanwhile, the University of Texas at Dallas discovered that learning new skills, such as photography or creative writing, improves memory and brain health, showing that our brains are malleable and capable of growth at any stage of life.

The key takeaway: the more you engage your mind, the more resilient and agile it becomes, ready to embrace the complexities of life with creativity and sharpness.

Beyond cognitive benefits, continuous learning fosters emotional resilience. Mastering new skills builds confidence and helps reduce stress, making you more equipped to handle life's challenges.

My Personal Journey of Continuous Learning and Personal Growth

Early in my career, I fell into the common trap of thinking that once formal education was over, the need for learning diminished. I worked hard, applying the knowledge I had gained in college, but over time, I felt a sense of stagnation—like I was going through the motions without any deeper sense of purpose or personal growth.

It wasn't until I attended a seminar led by Dr. Rakesh Arya that my mindset shifted. His presentation on *"How to Spend Every Minute Like a Dollar"* was a wake-up call. The way he broke down time management and personal productivity hit me hard, as I was overwhelmed by my business and personal life, leaving little room for self-improvement or new learning. His words gave me clarity and, more importantly, actionable steps that reignited my passion for learning.

I realised that learning wasn't confined to classrooms or textbooks—it was about expanding my understanding of how to better manage my life, my health, and my relationships. That seminar was a catalyst that led me to dive deeper into self-mastery, ultimately enrolling in Dr. Arya's course. Through that experience, I began reading more books on personal development, attending workshops, and constantly challenging myself to learn something new every day.

What I discovered was that embracing learning opened doors I didn't even know existed. With each new skill or piece of knowledge, I felt more equipped to face challenges and seize opportunities that I had previously overlooked. Since I have pursued continuous learning, I have been able to start a new business venture every year—ranging from warehousing and 3PL to insurance and real estate. The inspiration and confidence to write this book wouldn't have been possible without my commitment to continuous learning.

Through this journey, I didn't just acquire new skills; I transformed the way I approached challenges and opportunities. Each new venture, whether in business or personal development, was born out of my curiosity and willingness to keep learning. This ongoing pursuit of knowledge has been one of the most rewarding aspects of my life, and it continues to shape the person I am today.

"True growth isn't measured by how far you've come, but by how willing you are to keep learning along the way."

– Author

The Power of Continuous Learning: Richard Branson's Journey

Richard Branson, founder of the Virgin Group, is a living example of how embracing continuous learning leads to extraordinary success. Branson famously left school at 16 due to dyslexia and struggled in the traditional education system. But he never stopped learning. He sought knowledge through hands-on experiences, taking calculated risks, and learning from failures.

Branson attributes much of his success to his curiosity and willingness to continuously learn. From launching a student magazine to starting a record label and expanding into aviation and space travel, his career is a testament to how being open to new knowledge and experiences can lead to endless possibilities. He once said, *"You don't learn to walk by following rules. You learn by doing, and by falling over."*

Branson's hands-on approach to learning—through trial and error—shows that experience is often the best teacher. He didn't wait for formal education to guide him; he jumped in, learned by doing, and adapted with every new venture.

Like Branson, you can approach life with curiosity, see failure as a stepping stone, and remain open to learning in unexpected ways. Lifelong learning doesn't always require formal education—it's about seeking experiences that challenge and grow you.

Ask Yourself: *If Branson could overcome obstacles and thrive through hands-on learning, what's stopping you from doing the same?*

Key Components of Continuous Learning

1. **Curiosity**: Curiosity is the engine of lifelong learning. It drives you to explore the unknown, ask questions, and remain open to new possibilities. Curiosity not only fuels creativity but also keeps you engaged with the world.
2. **Adaptability**: In a rapidly evolving world, adaptability is essential. Lifelong learners embrace change and are willing to acquire new skills

to remain relevant. Being adaptable means you're never complacent; you're always ready to grow.

3. **Skill Development**: Continuously developing new skills—whether it's mastering a new language, learning how to code, or improving leadership abilities—builds your competence and opens doors to opportunities that wouldn't exist otherwise.
4. **Reflection**: Reflection is crucial for growth. By regularly assessing your experiences and learning from both successes and failures, you deepen your understanding of your strengths and areas for improvement.
5. **Networking and Collaboration**: Surround yourself with other learners. Building relationships with people who share your interests provides fresh perspectives, fosters creativity, and keeps you inspired on your learning journey.

"Education is the kindling of a flame, not the filling of a vessel."

– Socrates

The Tale of Two Woodchoppers: A Lesson in Continuous Growth

There's an old parable about two woodchoppers that perfectly illustrates the importance of continuous growth:

Two men went into the forest to chop wood. The first woodchopper worked tirelessly from morning until night, believing that hard work alone would yield the most results. However, as the day went on, his axe became dull, and his efforts slowed.

The second woodchopper, meanwhile, took regular breaks to sharpen his axe. While this may have seemed like wasted time to the first man, by the end of the day, the second woodchopper had felled more trees with less effort. His success wasn't because he worked harder, but because he worked smarter—he took the time to maintain his tools.

The lesson here is clear: continuous growth—sharpening your skills, reflecting on your progress, and taking time to improve—allows you to achieve more with less effort. Without stopping to "sharpen our axes," we risk burnout and reduced productivity.

In our fast-paced world, it's easy to get caught up in the hustle without taking the time to improve ourselves. But without investing in our own growth—whether that's learning new skills, taking care of our well-being, or reflecting on our actions—our success and happiness will eventually suffer.

Ask Yourself

1. What are the areas in your life where continuous learning would lead to personal or professional growth?
2. How can you build time for learning into your routine, even with a busy schedule?
3. What steps can you take to become more adaptable and open to new experiences?

Time to Take Action

1. **Create a Learning Action Plan**: Choose one specific skill or area of interest. Break it down into manageable steps.

   Example: If you want to learn a new language, start with downloading a language app or enrolling in an online class. Write down your timeline and commit to practising regularly.

2. **The 30-Day Challenge**: Commit to learning something new for 30 days. It could be reading a book on a subject you're unfamiliar with, watching educational videos, or even learning to cook new recipes. Document your journey, and reflect at the end of the month on how you've grown.

Final Thoughts

Embracing continuous learning is not just about gaining new skills; it's about cultivating a mindset that fuels growth, creativity, and adaptability. The journey to becoming your own superhero is lifelong, and learning is the path that will keep you moving forward, no matter where life takes you.

Much like Richard Branson, approach life with curiosity, seek out new experiences, and see challenges as opportunities to learn. Lifelong learning is the key to unlocking your potential and staying vibrant in mind and spirit.

The world is constantly changing, and your ability to evolve with it lies in your commitment to learning. Embrace it, seek it, and grow from it. Your inner superhero thrives when your mind is open, active, and ready to take on new challenges. Start today—the possibilities are endless.

Section 8

Skills for Success

Chapter 20

THE ART OF DELEGATION

"If you want to do a few small things right, do them yourself. If you want to do great things and make a big impact, learn to delegate."

– John C. Maxwell

Introduction to the Theme: The Power of Delegation

Delegation is not just a productivity tool; it's a key to unlocking the potential of others and achieving greater impact. Superheroes rely on their teams to achieve their missions—Batman has Alfred, the Avengers work together, and Superman often collaborates with the Justice League. Likewise, mastering the art of delegation allows you to focus on what you do best, while empowering others to contribute to the bigger picture. It's an essential skill for effective leadership, personal productivity, and growth.

Delegation doesn't stop at the office—it can improve your personal life as well. By delegating household tasks, such as grocery shopping or cleaning, to family members or external help, you free up time to focus on activities that bring you joy and relaxation.

"Great leaders don't do it all themselves; they empower others to do great things."

– Author

Be Your Own Superhero: Embracing Delegation

To be your own superhero, you need to harness the power of delegation. This involves recognizing what tasks you can delegate, selecting the right people for those tasks, and giving them the tools, authority, and trust to carry them out effectively. Delegation frees up your time to focus on strategic initiatives, reduces stress, and fosters a collaborative environment where everyone can contribute their strengths.

Imagine the Avengers without Iron Man's tech expertise or Captain America's leadership. Superheroes thrive because they leverage each other's strengths, not because one individual tries to do it all. Just like them, you too can amplify your success by trusting your team to play their part.

The Science Behind Delegation

Research supports the benefits of effective delegation in both leadership and productivity. A study published in the *Harvard Business Review* found that leaders who delegate effectively experience greater team engagement, higher productivity, and improved morale. Another study by the *American Psychological Association* found that proper delegation helps prevent burnout by distributing workloads evenly, reducing individual stress.

Delegation also fosters a culture of learning and growth within teams. When employees are trusted with responsibility, they gain confidence, improve their skills, and feel more connected to the organization's success. The result is a win-win situation where both the individual and the team grow together.

Key Components of Effective Delegation

1. **Identifying Delegable Tasks**: Start by determining which tasks are essential for you to handle personally, and which can be delegated. Focus on high-priority tasks that only you can manage, and delegate the rest to free up mental and physical bandwidth for strategic thinking.

2. **Selecting the Right People**: Choose team members who have the necessary skills, motivation, and potential for growth. Delegation is not just about offloading work—it's about empowering others to develop and take ownership.
3. **Providing Clear Instructions**: Clear communication is key to successful delegation. When assigning tasks, make sure to provide specific instructions, define the objectives, and set clear deadlines. This clarity reduces the risk of misunderstandings and ensures that everyone is on the same page.
4. **Empowering and Trusting**: Once you delegate a task, it's important to trust your team. Empower them by giving them the autonomy to make decisions and take ownership of the task. Micromanaging defeats the purpose of delegation.
5. **Monitoring and Feedback**: While delegation involves trust, it doesn't mean abdicating responsibility. Monitor progress, offer feedback, and provide support when needed. Regular check-ins ensure tasks stay on track and issues are addressed early.

The Challenge of Letting Go: My Personal Journey

Delegation, as simple as it sounds, has always been one of the toughest hurdles I've faced in my career. The fear of losing control was real, especially when it came to tasks that I believed only I could handle perfectly. I constantly hesitated, holding onto responsibilities as if they were delicate treasures that would break if passed to someone else. But this mindset nearly broke me.

In the early days of running my business, I was involved in everything—from marketing to operations. One task that I always insisted on doing myself was preparing freight proposals for clients to win their logistics contracts. This job required precision, as each freight proposal needed meticulous cost calculations which depended upon volume, type of product, source and destination, duration of the contract etc. With my growing business came an ever-increasing number of proposals. I found myself drowning in work. Long hours, late nights, and missed weekends became the norm. No matter how hard I worked, I was always behind, and opportunities were slipping through my fingers.

Yet, even as I struggled, I was reluctant to delegate. The thought of sharing sensitive information like costs and profit margins made me uncomfortable. What if my team made a mistake? What if they mishandled the data? What if we lost clients? What if they disclosed sensitive information to my competitors? All these "what ifs" haunted me until the unthinkable happened—I missed a deadline to submit my proposal for one of our biggest clients, a client we had worked with for over two decades. Losing that contract felt like a punch in the gut. That's when I realised my desire to control everything was costing me more than just time—it was costing me the success of my business.

After that blow, I had no choice but to change my approach. I made the difficult decision to delegate. Trust me, it wasn't smooth. It took time, patience, and a lot of faith in my team. I had to train them, share insights, and yes, even divulge the margins and costs I had been so protective of. But what happened next was nothing short of remarkable.

Not only did we begin hitting our deadlines again, but we also saw an increase in the number of proposals we could handle. The workload, which once seemed insurmountable, was now shared, and that allowed us to take on more contracts and expand our business. With delegation, I freed up my time, my mind, and my energy. Instead of staying stuck in daily tasks, I could finally focus on growing my business, strategizing for the future, and even exploring new ventures.

It took a near catastrophe for me to realise this, but delegating isn't about losing control—it's about gaining freedom. It's about trusting others to help you, to carry the load so that you can keep moving forward, growing, and achieving more than you ever could alone.

Delegation Isn't About Losing Control—It's About Empowering Others

Delegation is often misunderstood as losing control over tasks. In reality, it's about empowering others to contribute to your mission. By trusting others to handle certain responsibilities, you free yourself to focus on what truly matters—leading the vision and strategy. Effective delegation doesn't diminish your authority; it amplifies it by leveraging the collective skills of your team.

If you're hesitant to delegate, start by assigning smaller, less critical tasks. As you build confidence in your team's ability to handle responsibilities, gradually delegate more significant tasks. This phased approach helps you build trust while maintaining control over key areas.

"No person will make a great business who wants to do it all himself or get all the credit."

– Andrew Carnegie

The Pitfalls of Poor Delegation

When delegation is done poorly, it can create chaos instead of order. Dumping tasks on someone without clear direction, support, or accountability often leads to frustration, both for the delegator and the team. Poor delegation can result in mistakes, missed deadlines, and, ultimately, more work for you.

For instance, imagine a manager hurriedly offloading a task without proper explanation. The team member, unclear about the expectations, makes errors, forcing the manager to step back in and fix the problem. In the end, more time and effort are wasted than if the manager had simply handled the task from the start.

To avoid this, it's crucial to provide clear instructions, establish accountability, and ensure that everyone understands their roles and responsibilities. One useful tool for structured delegation is the **RACI Matrix**.

Using the RACI Matrix for Effective Delegation

The RACI Matrix (Responsible, Accountable, Consulted, Informed) is a simple framework that helps ensure tasks are delegated appropriately, with clear roles and responsibilities.

- **Responsible**: The individual who performs the task. They are in charge of getting the work done.
- **Accountable**: The person ultimately accountable for the task's success. They ensure it's completed correctly and on time.
- **Consulted**: People whose opinions or expertise are sought to inform decisions.
- **Informed**: Individuals who need to be kept updated on the task's progress or outcome.

Example of Delegation Using the RACI Framework

Let's say you're launching a new marketing campaign. Without a structured delegation framework, important details may be overlooked, and the campaign could fail to meet its objectives.

Using the RACI framework:

- **Responsible**: The marketing manager is responsible for executing the campaign.
- **Accountable**: You, as the business owner, are accountable for the campaign's success.
- **Consulted**: The sales team is consulted to ensure the campaign messaging aligns with customer needs.
- **Informed**: Your executive team is kept informed of the campaign's progress.

With this framework, everyone knows their role, accountability is clear, and communication flows smoothly, reducing the chance of missteps or delays.

Ask Yourself

1. What tasks in your workload can be delegated to others?
2. Who in your team has the potential to take on more responsibility?
3. How can you improve your communication and feedback when delegating tasks?

Time to Take Action

1. **Delegation Plan**: Identify tasks that can be delegated and assign them to the appropriate team members. Clearly outline the objectives, deadlines, and resources needed for each task.

2. **Feedback Loop**: Create a system for regular feedback and updates. Set up weekly or bi-weekly check-ins where team members can report progress and you can provide guidance and support.

Final Thoughts

Mastering the art of delegation is a critical step in becoming your own superhero. By effectively delegating tasks, empowering your team, and using structured frameworks like the RACI matrix, you can enhance productivity, reduce stress, and focus on strategic growth. Remember, delegation isn't about losing control—it's about empowering others to help you achieve your vision while multiplying your impact.

Delegation isn't just a tool for productivity—it's the key to sustainable success. By empowering others, you not only grow your business but also create a culture of collaboration and innovation that propels everyone forward.

Chapter 21

THE POWER OF SAYING NO

"It's only by saying no that you can concentrate on the things that are really important."

– Steve Jobs

Introduction to the Chapter's Theme: The Strength in Saying No

Saying no is an essential skill that many struggle to master. Just like superheroes face countless demands on their time, we, too, encounter endless requests in our personal and professional lives. Superheroes know when to set boundaries and prioritize their missions. In the same way, learning to say no allows us to maintain focus on our goals, reduce stress, and live a more intentional and fulfilling life.

"Saying no isn't a rejection of others—it's an affirmation of your priorities."

– Author

Be Your Own Superhero: Embracing the Power of Saying No

To be your own superhero, you need to understand the importance of saying no. This skill doesn't just preserve your time—it protects your energy, well-being, and mental health. Saying no allows you to focus on tasks that truly matter, aligned with your values and long-term objectives. Mastering the art of saying no enables you to live with purpose and clarity.

Just like Superman must choose his battles carefully, deciding when to step in and when to trust others, you, too, must prioritize your battles. Not every request requires your involvement—learning when to say no is what enables you to focus on the moments that truly matter.

The Science Behind Saying No

Studies show that the ability to say no directly correlates with better mental health and increased productivity. Research published in the *Journal of Consumer Research* reveals that people who say no to non-essential commitments experience significantly lower stress and higher life satisfaction. Similarly, the *American Psychological Association* emphasises that setting boundaries and prioritizing self-care prevents burnout and improves well-being.

Saying no reduces decision fatigue, allowing your brain to conserve energy for the things that really matter. It frees up cognitive resources, making you more efficient and focused.

The Dangers of Saying Yes to Everything

At first glance, always saying yes might seem heroic. However, as Spider-Man's story reveals, trying to do everything for everyone can take a massive toll. Peter Parker's constant battle to balance saving the world with managing his personal life often leaves him frazzled, unable to maintain strong relationships or prioritize his own well-being.

The same happens in our lives. When we say yes to everything, we become stretched thin—overwhelmed and burnt out. Every time we say yes to something that doesn't align with our priorities, we are effectively saying no to the things that do matter. Whether it's sacrificing family time, professional development, or even our mental health, the cost of saying yes can be far greater than we anticipate.

A Lesson from a Friend: Saket's Story

A story of my friend Saket perfectly illustrates the pitfalls of saying yes to everyone. One day, Saket received a call from Prachi, an old college friend, asking if he could help her friend Ruchi settle into Delhi after moving for a new job from Bangalore. Saket, known for never saying no, immediately agreed.

Over the next three days, Saket went above and beyond—picking Ruchi up from the airport, helping her find an apartment, negotiating with brokers, finalising a lease deed and assisting with furniture shopping. However, during this time, his own business suffered. By the fourth day, with work piling up, Saket finally asked for a break. To his surprise, Ruchi expressed disappointment that he wasn't more available and even complained to Prachi that Saket was being unhelpful.

When Saket shared this with me, I told him the issue wasn't Ruchi's reaction, but his inability to say no earlier. He had stretched himself too thin, leading to burnout and resentment. This happens to all of us when we prioritize others at the expense of our own needs. Saket learned a valuable lesson that saying no, early on, can prevent bigger problems down the line.

The Importance of Setting Boundaries

Learning to say no is not about being selfish—it's about self-preservation. When we constantly say yes to others, we often say no to ourselves. We all have limited time, energy, and mental resources, and when we give too much, we compromise our own well-being.

By setting clear boundaries, we protect our time and energy for the things that matter most—whether it's family, personal growth, or our professional goals. Saying no doesn't make you uncaring; it makes you intentional and allows you to give your best to what really matters.

Here are a few polite ways to say no without damaging relationships:

- 'I'm honoured that you thought of me, but I'm afraid I can't commit right now.'

- 'This sounds like a wonderful opportunity, but I'm currently focused on other priorities.'
- 'I'm flattered you asked, but I need to say no this time to honour my schedule.'

Mastering the Art of Saying No

Next time someone asks for your time or energy, pause and ask yourself: *Does this align with my goals and values?* If the answer is no, then feel empowered to decline. By saying no to what doesn't serve you, you create space for the things that truly matter.

Saying no doesn't always have to be harsh or blunt. It can be delivered with kindness, clarity, and respect. Remember, when you say yes to things that don't align with your priorities, you're essentially saying no to the things that could enrich your life.

Saying no doesn't have to burn bridges. A thoughtful response like, 'I appreciate the offer, but I need to focus on my current priorities,' or 'I'd love to help another time, but I'm fully committed right now,' can maintain relationships while protecting your time.

Key Components of Saying No

1. **Self-Awareness**: Recognise your limits and know when you are overcommitting. By cultivating self-awareness, you can identify when it's time to say no before you become overwhelmed.
2. **Setting Boundaries**: Establish clear boundaries and communicate them effectively. Knowing your non-negotiables allows you to confidently decline requests that don't align with your goals.
3. **Prioritizing**: Always prioritize based on your core values and long-term objectives. By focusing on your top priorities, you can more easily recognise what deserves your time and energy.
4. **Confident Communication**: Be direct and respectful when saying no. Clear communication helps others understand your decision without resentment or miscommunication.

5. **Managing Guilt**: Many people feel guilty when they say no. It's important to realise that saying no is a form of self-care. You are not obligated to please everyone at your own expense.

"When you say 'yes' to others, make sure you are not saying 'no' to yourself."

– Paulo Coelho

The Eisenhower Decision Matrix: A Tool for Prioritization

The Eisenhower Matrix is a simple yet powerful tool that helps categorize tasks based on their urgency and importance. It provides clarity when you're feeling overwhelmed with demands and requests. The matrix divides tasks into four quadrants:

1. **Do (Urgent and Important)**: Tasks that require immediate attention and have significant consequences if not completed. These are your top priorities.
2. **Decide (Important but Not Urgent)**: Tasks that are essential for long-term success but don't need immediate action. These tasks should be scheduled for later.
3. **Delegate (Urgent but Not Important)**: Tasks that need to be done but don't require your personal attention. These can be delegated to others to free up your time for more meaningful work.
4. **Delete (Not Urgent and Not Important)**: These tasks don't add value to your goals and can be eliminated. These distractions should be minimized or avoided.

Applying the Eisenhower Matrix to My Life

The first time I applied the Eisenhower Matrix, I was surprised to see how many of my daily tasks were neither urgent nor important. Once I categorized my work, I delegated unnecessary tasks and focused on high-impact activities that aligned with my long-term goals. The matrix not only increased my productivity but also reduced my stress by allowing me to focus on what really mattered.

But one of the biggest changes came when I learned to say *no* to the tasks that fell into the "Delete" category—tasks that weren't important or urgent. These were the time-consuming distractions that added no real value to my business or personal life. For years, I had unknowingly allowed these tasks to clutter my day, stealing time and energy that I could have invested elsewhere. Whether it was unnecessary meetings, random requests, or unproductive habits, I realised that by constantly saying "yes," I was overburdening myself with responsibilities that had no impact on my goals.

Saying "no" was tough at first, especially for someone who prided themselves on being available and involved. But over time, I saw the immense benefits. It wasn't just about freeing up my schedule—it was about reclaiming control of my life. By saying *no* to distractions, I could fully commit to the areas that truly needed my attention, whether it was growing my business or spending quality time with family. This shift transformed my approach to time management and allowed me to focus on what really mattered, achieving greater balance and fulfillment in both my professional and personal life.

Ask Yourself

1. What are your current limits, and how do you recognise when you're taking on too much?
2. How can you set and communicate clear boundaries in both your personal and professional life?
3. What are your top priorities, and how can you ensure your commitments align with them?

Time to Take Action

1. **Boundaries Map**: Draw a boundaries map for different aspects of your life (work, relationships, personal time). Define what's acceptable and non-negotiable in each area.
2. **No Practice**: Practice saying no in role-playing scenarios with a friend or mentor. This will help you build confidence and learn to decline requests respectfully but firmly.

Final Thoughts

Learning to say no is not just about protecting your time; it's about taking control of your life. By setting boundaries, prioritizing your goals, and confidently declining requests that don't serve you, you protect your energy for what truly matters. Embracing the power of saying no is a fundamental step in becoming your own superhero, enabling you to lead a more focused, intentional, and fulfilling life.

Saying no isn't about limitation—it's about liberation. It frees you to pursue your purpose, nurture your well-being, and focus on what truly lights you up.

Chapter 22

THE POWER OF DOING NOTHING

"By doing nothing, everything is done."

– Lao Tzu

Introduction to the Theme: The Importance of Rest and Reflection

In a world that constantly glorifies busyness and productivity, the idea of "doing nothing" might seem counterproductive, even absurd. However, even the strongest superheroes need moments of rest to maintain their powers and gain clarity on their missions. Similarly, we must understand the value of pausing and embracing stillness. In doing so, we allow our minds and bodies to recharge, foster creativity, and enhance our overall well-being.

Doing nothing doesn't mean sitting idly; it means allowing space for your mind to wander, reflect, and rejuvenate. It's about being intentional with your downtime to restore energy and creativity.

This chapter will guide you on how to master the art of stillness and reflection—helping you find balance in a fast-paced world and enabling you to become your own superhero.

"In the stillness of doing nothing, you create space for everything."

– Author

Be Your Own Superhero: Embracing the Power of Doing Nothing

To be your own superhero, you must recognise the importance of intentional rest and reflection. Doing nothing doesn't mean being idle or lazy. It means creating the space to reset, reflect, and replenish your energy. By carving out moments to "just be," you'll be able to return to your goals with renewed focus, creativity, and clarity.

Even Batman has his Batcave—a place where he withdraws from the world to strategize and recover after each battle. Just like him, we all need a retreat where we can pause, reflect, and recharge.

Doing nothing is not a waste of time; it's an investment in yourself and your well-being.

The Science Behind Doing Nothing

Resting and allowing your mind to wander is essential for both mental and physical health. Research in *Psychological Science* found that when we take breaks and let our minds rest, we experience a boost in creativity and problem-solving. Another study by the *American Psychological Association* highlighted that regular periods of rest improve memory, reduce stress, and enhance overall life satisfaction.

Taking the time to do nothing, whether through mindfulness, daydreaming, or quiet reflection, allows your brain to process information more effectively. It's in those moments of rest that your subconscious mind begins to connect ideas, generate solutions, and provide insights.

A Personal Lesson: Rediscovering the Power of Rest

For years, I believed that productivity was the ultimate measure of success. I broke down my entire day into 15-minute tasks, leaving no room for rest. From the moment I woke up to the time I went to bed, every minute was packed with activities I felt I *had* to complete. If, by chance, I missed a task during the week, I would carry it over to Sunday, which soon became a day of relentless catch-up.

Sundays were no longer a day of rest. They had transformed into an extension of the workweek—filled with errands, meetings, and obligations. I was so focused on getting everything done that I didn't realise how much this constant activity was taking a toll on me. I would often find myself physically exhausted and mentally drained, and the joy I used to feel from accomplishments was replaced by a sense of overwhelm.

Then, one day, a memory from my childhood surfaced. Growing up in Mumbai, Sundays were sacred in our household. After 12 pm, my family would switch off the doorbell so that no one could disturb us. No one called, no one visited. Sundays were days of pure rest. We would enjoy a leisurely breakfast, switch off from the world, and spend the day together as a family. Those days were filled with calm, laughter, and a sense of togetherness that seemed to fade as I grew older.

Inspired by this memory, I made a bold decision: I reclaimed my Sundays. I stopped packing them with leftover tasks and instead designated them as sacred, unstructured days. No meetings, no work, no errands. If I wanted to go for a walk, read a book, or simply sit in silence, I would—but by choice, not obligation.

Now, Sundays are like a boat with no rudder or sail, slowly drifting through the ocean, driven by the winds, like grains of sand slowly slipping from my fingers in peace.

The shift was profound. By allowing myself to rest, I found myself gaining more—more clarity, more joy, more energy. The constant pressure to *do* vanished, and I rediscovered the balance I had long lost. I stopped associating productivity with self-worth, realizing that taking time to rest wasn't laziness—it was essential for my well-being.

When was the last time you allowed yourself to be still, without any agenda? Doing nothing is not about wasting time, but about giving your mind and spirit the space to restore. It's about making room for what truly matters. Sometimes, in order to move forward, we first need to pause.

Key Components of Doing Nothing

1. **Rest and Recovery**: True rest—physical, mental, and emotional—is crucial for maintaining long-term energy and focus. This kind of recovery allows your body and mind to repair and rejuvenate.
2. **Mindfulness and Presence**: Mindfulness is the practice of staying present in the moment. By focusing on the here and now, without distraction, you can reduce stress and enhance your awareness.
3. **Reflection and Insight**: Reflection is a powerful tool for personal growth. By taking time to reflect on your experiences, thoughts, and emotions, you gain deeper insight into your own life and decisions.
4. **Unstructured Time**: Scheduling time where you don't have to "do" anything allows for spontaneous creativity and relaxation. It's a space free from obligations where you can recharge.
5. **Embracing Silence**: In a world filled with noise and distractions, silence is a rare but powerful tool. Embracing moments of silence allows you to reconnect with your inner self and find peace.

The Power of Doing Nothing in Practice

For many of us, the idea of doing nothing may feel uncomfortable, even guilt-inducing. We're often conditioned to equate rest with laziness, but nothing could be further from the truth. Consider the story of Bill Gates, one of the most successful business leaders in the world. Gates is known for taking "think weeks"—periods of time where he disconnects from work, isolates himself from distractions, and simply reflects.

During one of these "think weeks," Gates came up with the idea for Internet Explorer, which later became a pivotal product for Microsoft. His moments of stillness and reflection allowed him to see the big picture and think creatively about future innovations.

This is the power of intentional rest. It's not just about relaxing—it's about creating the mental space for breakthroughs.

Reflection is where the magic happens. It's when you pause to look back, connect dots, and gain deeper insight into your journey. By creating time for regular reflection, you allow space for personal growth and clarity about your next steps.

"You cannot always control what goes on outside. But you can always control what goes on inside."

– Wayne Dyer

Ask Yourself

1. How do you currently incorporate rest and relaxation into your daily routine?
2. What activities make you feel most present and mindful?
3. How can you create more unstructured time in your schedule for reflection and rest?

Time to Take Action

1. **Mindfulness Meditation**: Dedicate 5-10 minutes each day to mindfulness meditation. Focus on your breath and observe your thoughts without judgment. This practice can help centre your mind and reduce stress.

2. **Unplugged Retreat**: Plan a mini-retreat for yourself, whether for a few hours or an entire day. Disconnect from technology and spend this time in silence and solitude. Use this time to reconnect with yourself and your inner peace.

Call to Action: Finding Balance in Rest

In a world where we're constantly chasing goals, it's easy to forget the value of rest. But remember, even the most powerful superheroes know the importance of taking a break to recharge.

This week, challenge yourself to schedule “doing nothing” into your life. Whether it’s 15 minutes a day or an entire Sunday, make the commitment to rest and reflect. You might be surprised by the clarity and creativity that emerges from those moments of stillness.

Final Thoughts

The power of doing nothing is not about laziness—it’s about intentional rest and reflection. By allowing yourself time to pause, be present, and recharge, you can improve your overall well-being, enhance your creativity, and regain focus. In both your personal and professional life, this balance is key to long-term success and happiness. Embrace the art of doing nothing, and watch how it transforms your life for the better.

Doing nothing is a practice—a muscle you strengthen over time. The more you allow yourself these moments of rest, the more you’ll discover clarity, creativity, and balance in your life.

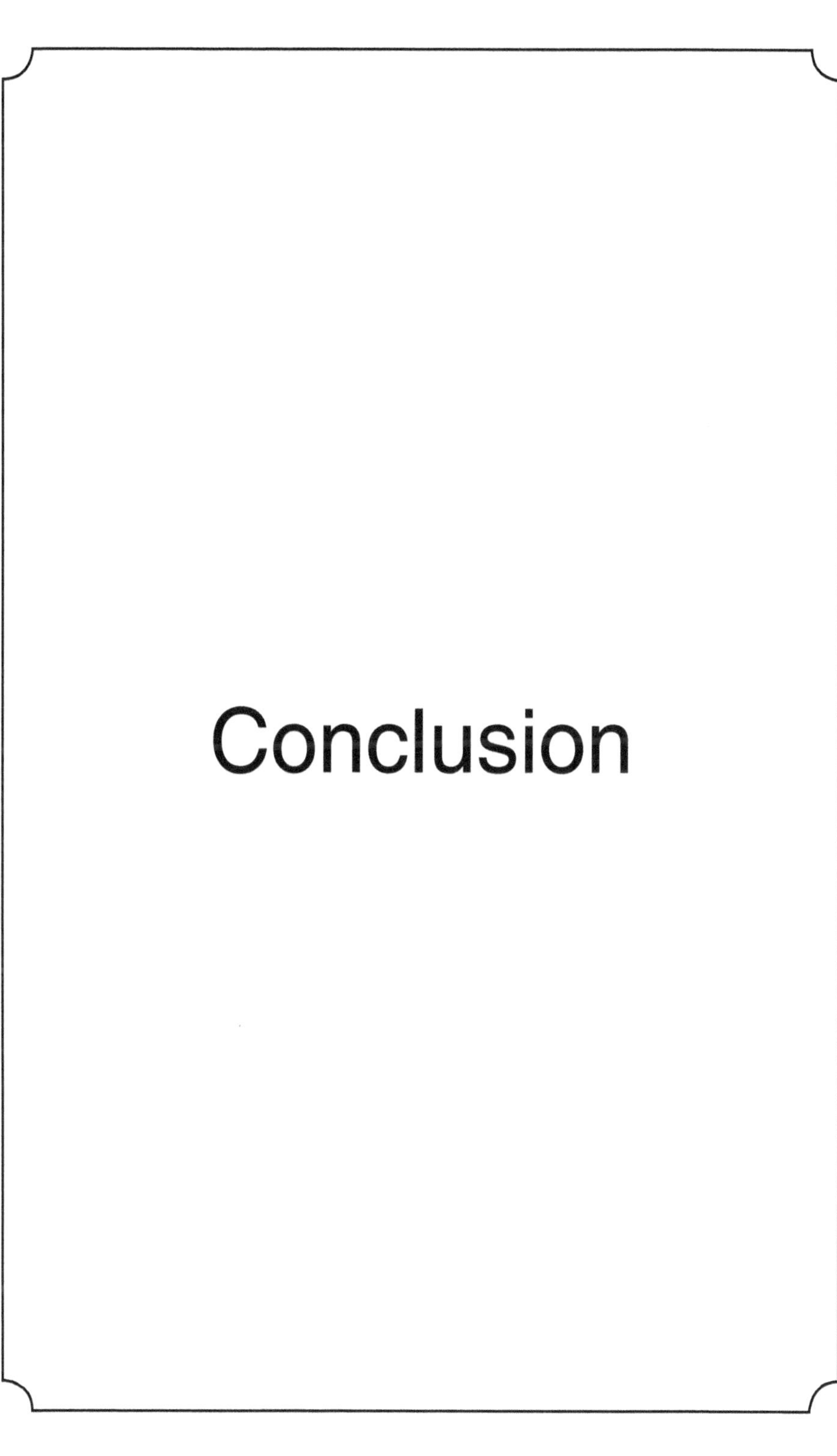

Conclusion

Chapter 23

CONCLUSION – EMBRACE YOUR INNER SUPERHERO

"The journey of a thousand miles begins with one step."

– Lao Tzu

The Journey of Transformation

Throughout this book, we've explored powerful principles that are designed to help you unlock your inner superhero. From cultivating a positive mindset to mastering the art of time management, each chapter has been a stepping stone in the journey toward holistic living and self-improvement. Now that you've completed this part of your journey, it's time to recognise one important truth: transformation is not a destination—it's a lifelong process.

This chapter serves as a reminder that true transformation requires more than just absorbing information. It demands **action**—the courage to implement the insights and lessons you've learned. While knowledge is the foundation, implementation is the key that turns potential into reality. As we bring this book to a close, remember: **It is not information but implementation that leads to transformation.**

Embrace Your Inner Superhero

Becoming your own superhero means stepping up to take full responsibility for your life, your choices, and your growth. It's about more than just gathering knowledge—it's about using that knowledge to create real, tangible change. The tools and strategies you've learned in this book are your superpowers. But like any superhero, your powers are only effective when you use them.

Superheroes are defined not by their abilities, but by their actions. Similarly, it's not what you know that will define your life; it's what you *do* with that knowledge. Each step you take, no matter how small, moves you closer to your goals. The true power of transformation lies not in grand gestures but in the daily, incremental actions that shape your future.

Embracing your inner superhero doesn't mean you need superpowers—it means recognizing the power you already have to change your life. Just like a superhero takes on challenges one battle at a time, you conquer your goals one step at a time. Your power lies in your choices, in how you respond to life, and in the actions you take daily. Each decision you make is a heroic act that moves you closer to your dreams.

"A superhero's greatest power isn't their strength—it's their decision to act despite fear or uncertainty."

– Author

My personal story

Years ago, I found myself at a crossroads in my life. I had all the knowledge I needed—countless self-help books, courses, and motivational talks—but I wasn't seeing any significant change. Why? Because I hadn't taken the next step. I hadn't applied what I'd learned consistently.

I remember standing at the edge of change, filled with doubt. Despite all the knowledge I had accumulated, I feared that the steps I took wouldn't be enough to make a difference. But what I realised was that action, even imperfect action, creates momentum. Once I started applying what I had learned—even in small doses—the change became inevitable.

Once I began implementing those principles—once I took action—everything started to shift. Small steps turned into big leaps, and soon, I was living the balanced, fulfilling life I had once only imagined.

Key Takeaways: The Journey to Abundance

As you reflect on the lessons from this book, here are the essential takeaways that will guide you toward a life of abundance and fulfillment:

1. **Mindset and Mental Health:** Your mindset shapes your reality. Cultivating self-awareness, healing from past wounds, and developing a positive outlook are the foundation for mental clarity and emotional resilience.
2. **Physical Health and Wellness:** Your body is your most valuable asset. Prioritize your physical health through proper nutrition, regular exercise, and mental well-being to create a balanced and sustainable lifestyle.
3. **Relationships and Community:** Relationships are your emotional anchor. Surround yourself with people who uplift and inspire you, and nurture meaningful connections that foster personal growth and emotional support.
4. **Goal Setting and Personal Growth:** Success begins with setting clear, intentional goals. Embrace a growth mindset, continuously learn, and pursue your passions to build a life of purpose and achievement.
5. **Balance and Time Management:** Time is your most precious resource. Learn to balance work, relationships, and personal well-being by mastering time management and regularly assessing your progress.
6. **Productivity and Proactivity:** Overcome procrastination and develop habits that promote proactivity. Structured systems, discipline, and actionable plans lead to sustainable success.
7. **Gratitude and Growth:** Practicing gratitude creates a positive outlook on life, while a commitment to personal growth keeps you evolving into the best version of yourself.

8. **Leadership and Delegation:** As you lead your life or team, remember the power of delegation. Empower others, set boundaries, and focus on what truly matters.

The Missing Link: From Information to Implementation

We live in a world where information is abundant—self-help books, motivational videos, online courses—but transformation doesn't happen simply by knowing more. True transformation happens when you **implement** what you've learned. Information is potential power; **implementation is actual power**.

Think about it: You've probably read numerous articles on goal-setting, time management, or mindfulness. But how often have you taken what you've learned and consistently applied it in your daily life? This is the moment where most people fall short. They gather knowledge but fail to take action.

It's not enough to know the steps to change. You must take them.

Call to Action: The Power of the First Step

As this book comes to a close, it's time to take that first step. The first step toward implementing what you've learned. Taking the first step can often be the hardest—it's where fear, doubt, and uncertainty all try to hold you back. But it's also where the magic begins. The hardest part of the journey is often simply starting, but once you take that step, each subsequent one gets easier. Your journey toward greatness begins the moment you choose to move.

Change doesn't have to happen all at once. Start with small, manageable actions. Whether it's setting a new goal, starting a mindfulness practice, or creating a daily routine, every small action brings you closer to the life you desire.

Remember, you don't need to have everything figured out. Superheroes don't always know how they'll defeat the villain—they just know they have to take the first step toward victory. **That's where transformation begins.**

"The power to change your life isn't hidden in knowledge—it's found in the actions you take every single day."

– Author

Ask Yourself

1. Which principles from this book resonate with you the most, and why?
2. How can you begin to implement these principles in your daily life?
3. What small action can you take today to move toward the life you envision?

Taking Action on Your Journey

1. **Action Plan Creation**: Choose one area of your life (health, relationships, career, or personal growth) and create a simple, actionable plan to improve it. Break your goal into small, daily steps that you can start implementing today.

   Tip: Whether it's as simple as drinking a glass of water first thing in the morning or taking 5 minutes to meditate before work, the power of transformation starts small. You don't need to leap—you just need to step forward.

2. **30-Day Implementation Challenge**: Select one principle from this book and commit to implementing it consistently for 30 days. Whether it's practicing gratitude, setting boundaries, or delegating tasks, track your progress and reflect on the impact this change has on your life.

The Journey Continues

As we come to the end of this book, I want to leave you with one final thought: **You are your own superhero.**

Transformation is not something that happens overnight—it is the result of consistent, intentional action. The principles you've learned here are powerful, but their true impact will only be felt when you put them into practice. You have the tools, the knowledge, and the strength within you. Now, all that's left is for you to take that first step.

Your journey doesn't end here—it begins here.

"There is no passion to be found playing small—in settling for a life that is less than the one you are capable of living."

– Nelson Mandela

Final Thoughts

As you stand here, at the end of this book, remember that this is only the beginning. You've already done the hard work by seeking out knowledge and insights. Now, it's time to trust yourself to take the next step. You already have what it takes to become the superhero of your own life. The world needs what you have to offer—your unique strength, your courage, your vision. So go forward with confidence, take action, and live boldly. Your greatest adventure is just beginning.

Thank you for embarking on this journey toward mastering life through holistic living and personal growth. May this book serve as your guide and companion as you continue to embrace your inner champion. The power to transform your life is within you—don't just seek information, seek transformation. **Take action, live with purpose, and inspire others along the way.**

The world is waiting for your greatness. Now go, **be your own superhero**.

ABOUT THE AUTHOR

Amit Agarwal is a dynamic entrepreneur with over two decades of experience in fields as diverse as transportation, logistics, real estate, and insurance. Since graduating from N M College, Mumbai, in 2002, Amit has expanded his family business from a single operation to over 36 locations across India, moving into logistics warehousing and 3PL services. Beyond his entrepreneurial pursuits, he also serves as an insurance agent with TATA AIG and is a real estate developer in the Delhi NCR region.

After stepping into his father's business, Amit initially found himself feeling stuck, both professionally and personally. He was hoping for a savior to bring change but soon realized that only he could truly transform his life. This realization marked the beginning of Amit's journey of self-discovery and personal transformation—a journey that laid the foundation for his first book. He encountered many others like him—wonderful, capable individuals who were living life without a clear goal or passion, often feeling lost or limited. Writing this book was his way of extending a helping hand to those who, like him, sought direction and growth. His hope is that this book helps readers design their own lives and achieve greatness on their own terms.

Amit's personal philosophy centers on mental resilience and positivity: *"Your mind is the most valuable real estate you will ever own; don't let negativity acquire it."* His work encourages readers to cultivate a positive, growth-oriented mindset as the key to unlocking their inner potential. Through *Unlock Your Inner Superhero: Practical Steps for Holistic Living and Personal Mastery,* Amit aims to inspire readers to become who they were truly meant to be, leading lives filled with purpose, joy, and fulfillment.

Dedicated to continuous learning and fitness, Amit places high importance on physical well-being and loves playing badminton. In addition to his business pursuits, he is an active philanthropist, supporting causes close to his heart such as education and healthcare. He is actively involved with various schools, colleges, and hospitals as a patron and trustee, working to make a positive impact in these vital areas.

Amit's contributions to the business world have been widely recognized, including accolades like *"Transportation and Logistics Business of the Year"* by Franchise India, Times Now, and Entrepreneur Magazine in 2017, and "20 Most Promising Hire Carrier Service Providers" by Silicon India Magazine in 2019.

Currently based in Delhi, Amit enjoys music, traveling, and reading. He is already working on his next book, focusing on time management—a skill he believes is crucial for reclaiming control over one's life.

Stay Connected with Amit Agarwal

Thank you for taking the journey through Unlock Your Inner Superhero. I would love to hear your thoughts, insights, and experiences as you embark on your own path to personal growth and holistic living. Join me across platforms, and let's continue to inspire each other to achieve greatness.

Connect with me:

Instagram – For daily inspiration and insights:
instagram.com/_amitagarwal__/

LinkedIn – Connect professionally for updates and discussions:
linkedin.com/in/amittransport/

YouTube – Watch videos on personal growth, business, and more:
youtube.com/@officialamitagarwal

Website – Visit for blogs, resources, and upcoming events:
amitagarwal.one

Email – I'd love to hear from you directly:
amit.agarwal@amittransport.com

Stay connected, stay inspired, and let's unlock greatness together!

www.ingramcontent.com/pod-product-compliance
Lightning Source LLC
LaVergne TN
LVHW021138160826
845679LV00023B/1951
9798895886137